CAN YOU SEE THE CROSS FROM THERE?

GRACE AND GRIT FOR SUFFERERS AND SINNERS

TERRY POWELL

May whoever reads this find encouragement and comfort from God's Word that I explain herein. Terry Powell

10-8-24

terry.powell @ cıu.edu

803-673-0231

SERVESTRONG
PUBLISHING

Columbia, South Carolina

Can You See The Cross From There?: Grace and Grit For Sufferers and Sinners

Unless otherwise indicated, Scripture quotations are from the ESV Bible (The Holy Bible, English Standard Version), copyright 2001 by Crossway, a publishing ministry of Good News Publishers. 2011 Text Edition. All rights reserved.

Typeset by Doug Serven

Cover design by Sean Benesh

Paperback ISBN: 978-0-9971796-1-3

To contact the author, email him at terry.powell@ciu.edu

WHY READ THIS BOOK?

A few of the questions that frame the content of this book:

- What obscures your view of the cross, keeping you from seeing and appropriating the benefits of Jesus' death?
- How is it possible that God manifests His glory best through your weaknesses and needs?
- When you suffer, what Bible truths and divine attributes offer heart-massaging comfort?
- When you sin, do you picture Christ wearing a frown and pointing a long index finger at you? Or is He smiling at you with wide-open arms, yearning for you to come to Him?
- What would personal spiritual revival look like for you?
- Which better facilitates holiness: teeth-gritting effort or falling more in love with the Savior?

- What is self-defeating about looking to other people or your accomplishments to sculpt your personal identity and instill a sense of significance?
- How can you replace the harmful, critical things you say to yourself with life-changing self-talk based on God's Word?
- Do prayers of lament—approaching God with doubts, honest venting and tough questions—reveal a lack of faith in Him, or evidence of it?
- What's required of you before others in the body of Christ can help bear your burdens?

Through glimpses of my personal pilgrimage and inner life as a Christian, my prayer is that you'll see yourself and the realistic nature of living as a Christian in a fallen world. The late author Henri Nouwen believed that Christian writing that's transparent and personal has universal application for the larger body of Christ: "What is most personal and unique in each of us is probably the very element which would, if shared or expressed, speak most deeply to others."[1]

As you read, listen closely to what the Savior wants to say to you.

TO STEPHEN FLOYD POWELL

I respect and admire you more than you realize.

For your resilience as a weightlifting coach despite dealing with Asperger syndrome. For diligence as a lifelong learner when it comes to fitness, nutrition and weightlifting performance. For your incisive thinking concerning social issues, political platforms and the application of biblical teaching in a post-Christian culture. For your tender heart toward dogs, demonstrated in your ownership of two dachshunds, plus your rescue of strays who received a new lease on life with new owners. And for coaxing me in 2007 to stop talking about getting a dachshund and commit to one.

You're also an extraordinary up-front communicator. I watched in awe as you led a workshop on weightlifting technique for state high school strength coaches. You didn't *tell* them what to do with their athletes—you *showed* them, utilizing an on-site lifter and video clips from a renowned coach in China. What passion you demonstrated! What a reservoir of knowledge and anecdotes you conveyed! I prayed, "Oh Lord, enable me to teach with this kind of fervor and skill!"

Stephen, I haven't always loved you intelligently, but I've always loved you passionately. I'm proud to be your dad and I yearn to become a closer friend in my latter years.

PRAISE FOR CAN YOU SEE THE CROSS FROM THERE?

This Scripture-laced devotional is theologically rich and insightful. Terry offers readers solid encouragement, unflinching honesty, penetrating prayers and memorable quotes on each topic he covers. You will want a highlighter as you read this outstanding book!
—Vaneetha Risner
Author of *The Scars That Have Shaped Me* and *Walking Through Fire: A Memoir of Loss and Redemption*

Over the years, I've been tremendously blessed by Terry's commitment to magnifying Christ in the midst of his weakness. In this new resource, he encourages others to do the same as they press forward through the Christian life. Through poetic expressions and thoughtful reflections, readers learn how to engage their Savior with their troubles while considering what God would have them learn in the process. This book will be a sanctifying tool in the hands of those who want to know God better as well as understand themselves.
—Christine Chappell
Author of *Midnight Mercies: Walking with God through Depression in Motherhood* and *Help! I've Been Diagnosed with a Mental Disorder*; Certified Biblical Counselor

Terry's personal reflections, faith poems, Bible input and probing application questions planted gospel seeds in my heart as I delved into his new book. Continually I was reminded of the inside-out phenomenon of a life transformed by the Holy Spirit's power. While I was reading his manuscript my earthly pilgrimage took an unexpected turn when God took my husband up to heaven. Many insights from Terry's book enabled me to endure one of the greatest trials of my life by shifting my focus to God's grace and the grit He can give us to handle affliction. Also, I gleaned from his book an arm-full of apt quotes that helped me for the path I'm on.

I wholeheartedly commend this book for all who desire to view the cross of Christ and its benefits clearly.

—Delaine Blackwell
Founder of *Joy Abiding, Inc.* and Teaching Director for Community Bible Study in South Carolina

This book is full of short, readable chapters that point its readers to the joy of appropriating the benefits of Jesus' cross. Terry explains Bible truths clearly and accurately. He's transparent in describing his struggles as well as illustrating the sources of his comfort. What he writes is both helpful and restorative. Terry comes alongside the reader and shares the grace he has received from God in dealing with personal areas of suffering and his ongoing fight against what he calls "the indwelling sin of believers." Read this and fill up on the refreshing water of the Lord's grace that has been bountifully poured out in Terry's life.

—Howard Blomberg
Church Elder, founder of *The Handyman Helper*

Real. Raw. Restorative. Those are the words that describe Terry's book. The personal anecdotes he shares resonate with me because they help me apply the Bible truths he explains in a way that only narrative and experiences can. Terry has a gift of identifying with the broken, hurt, and discouraged while also pointing them to our Savior and what He did for us on the cross. Throughout it he provides personal stories, original poetry, biblical meditations, prayers and quotes from well-known authors that make for interesting reading. I highly recommend this book!

—Jonah Fair
Youth Pastor and Counselor

I've thanked the Lord many times for the gift of being able to read this book at this particular point in my spiritual journey. The Bible truths, illustrations, heartfelt poems, reflective questions and prayers remind me that God is with me in my suffering and He can accomplish His purposes through it. It's the kind of book you can read a chapter "a la carte," based on how a chapter title resonates with you. Or you can read it straight through, a chapter a day for 31 days, as a more-extensive-than-usual devotional resource. Terry shares areas of personal pain and weakness, yet there is triumph in these pages since he shows how reliance on God's grace gets him through it all.

—Lynn Thompson

Terry's book is encouraging to anyone in the midst of struggle, especially to the person who walks in emotional darkness. I was challenged and instructed by it because he provides helpful and hopeful counsel for our Christian walk, with an emphasis on how God's grace sustains us in our hardships and enables us to handle sin appropriately. The book teems with vital truths concerning how we can view the cross of Christ from any life situation we are experiencing. Each chapter contains helpful biblical advice, original poetry, thoughtful questions and multiple Bible verses on the theme. Whether you're dealing with a sin problem, an obedience struggle, a ministry dilemma or an emotional crisis, you'll find practical ways to handle these concerns. And Terry will consistently point you to the finished work of Jesus on the cross.

—Melissa Schneck
Pastor's wife and Bible study leader

I love the **Prayer Response** in each chapter and the bounty of encouraging, heart-lifting Scriptures! We're flooded with books in this tech age, but not many contain such rich substance. I include Terry's book in the caliber of books still in print written by saints from past eras. It's an unusual, in-depth devotional book that both challenges and comforts.

—Melody Bollinger
Author of *Loved One: An Invitation to Feel God's Love and to Experience His Desire to be Your God-Sized Help*

Terry faithfully exegetes God's Word and shares how he has experienced the sustenance of the Lord in dealing with issues such as major depression and discouraging circumstances. I appreciate his emphasis on the glory of God and how we can honor God by how we respond to both internal and external stressors. Even if you've never experienced depression, you'll discover strategies that will assist you in other areas of struggle, plus you'll learn how to respond graciously to those who are prone to discouragement.

—Wade Hobbs, PhD
Missionary and former pastor

I loved every word of *Can You See the Cross from There?* Terry Powell is a theologian, poet and heart surgeon who the Holy

Spirit uses throughout this book to give me greater vision of the Lord and His calling on my life. I have an entire page of notes citing insights that spoke to me. I plan on reading this book over and over again. This book is for anyone who is seeking to go deeper with the Lord in the midst of current struggles. It will challenge you. Encourage you. Strengthen your faith and enhance your intimacy with the Lord. It will make you laugh one minute and cry the next. Terry's poetry and insights will inspire your heart and increase appreciation for your Savior. Thank you, Terry, for a book that stretches my faith in the midst of the Lord doing necessary heart surgery on me!

—Tim Hanley

Ordained Pastor in the Presbyterian Church in America, founder of *One Church Ablaze*, an evangelistic and training ministry for encouraging revival in the church

CONTENTS

ACKNOWLEDGMENTS

Though writing requires a lot of solitary endeavor, many persons contributed significantly to the process and final version of this book.

Hope Chenault typed numerous revisions of the manuscript and served as an eagle-eye copy editor. She also recommended insightful changes in word choices and taught me to think like the readers I desire to reach.

Greta Clinton suggested major format and content changes that resulted in a tighter, more appealing, reader-friendly appearance to each chapter.

A number of advanced readers gave encouraging feedback as well as concrete suggestions that motivated me during the inevitable but tedious revisions of the initial manuscript. A well-deserved "Thank you!" to Howard Blomberg, Maria Cochrane, Jonah Fair, Wade Hobbs, Lynn Thompson, Wanda Parks, Melissa Schneck, Delaine Blackwell, Christine Chappell, Vaneetha Risner, Melody Bollinger and Tim Hanley.

I appreciate the fine work of Doug Serven, a local church pastor and founder of Storied Publishing, for coming up with the book cover and interior design.

A number of special people often prayed for me during the two-year writing process: my bride, Dolly, and in addition to persons already named on this page, Mark McCann, Lynn Hoekstra and David Cashin.

I'd be remiss if I didn't acknowledge Columbia International University, where I taught full-time in Church Ministry for 38 years. I especially thank the two deans in the Seminary and School of Ministry for allowing me to use an office full-time for four years after I retired in 2019: Dr. John Harvey and Dr. David Croteau. That's where I did the majority of spade work and manuscript revisions.

Yet no one deserves more gratitude than my Savior, Jesus Christ. His unconditional love for me, demonstrated most vividly by His sacrificial death on the cross, has sustained me ever since my childhood, when I first believed in Him. *Oh, may I keep seeing the cross and its benefits clearly!*

A HYMN: WHEN I SURVEY THE WONDROUS CROSS

ISAAC WATTS, 1674—1748

When I survey the wondrous Cross
On which the Prince of Glory died,
My richest gain I count but loss,
And pour contempt on all my pride.

Forbid it, Lord, that I should boast,
Save in the death of Christ my God:
All the vain things that charm me most,
I sacrifice them to his blood.

See from his head, his hands, his feet,
Sorrow and love flow mingled down!
Did ever such love and sorrow meet?
Or thorns compose so rich a crown?

Were the whole realm of nature mine,
That were a present far too small;
Love so amazing, so divine,
Demands my soul, my life, my all.

INTRODUCTION

This book consists of original faith poems, along with personal experiences and biblical teachings that inspired the lyrics. My approach is personal and transparent, not sterile or theoretical. What you'll read emanates from my heart, not only my mind. Challenges and stressors I've faced as a Christ-follower, and the means I've used to stand up to them, stitch together the various topics and chapters.

Every Christian faces difficulties, both internal and external. Perhaps one or more of the challenges to faith and fruitfulness I've experienced will resonate with you: relentless temptation and other forms of spiritual warfare; low self-image; insecure personal identity; recurring episodes of major depression*; an achievement-oriented basis for personal significance; false guilt (forgetting I'm forgiven); harsh, condemning self-talk; threats that try to sabotage relationships—just to name a few.

The poems and meditations illustrate how I employ those resources and spiritual practices. I want to encourage you and to equip you to overcome the inevitable challenges you face to spiritual formation and usefulness to Christ.

The Book's Title

I'm using the term *cross* in the title as a figure of speech.

A *metonymy* is the use of one word in place of another term that it represents. For example, the term "press" stands for a group of journalists covering a newsworthy event. A restaurant that promotes "surf and turf" offers menu items that combine seafood and beef.

> **"**
> I want to encourage you and to equip you to overcome the inevitable challenges you face to spiritual formation and usefulness to Christ.
> **"**

In one form of metonymy, the word is only a component of, or a part of, whatever is being characterized. It's when a part of something stands for the whole. For example, "all *hands* on deck" refers to the full slate of laborers who start work on a ship. When we inquire about a friend's new "wheels," we're referring to his car.

The *cross* in the title stands for the entire Christian gospel. In Galatians 6:14, Paul used the word in the same way. In contrast to persons who boasted in the flesh, he said, "Far be it for me to boast except in the cross of our Lord Jesus Christ."

Paul wasn't referring to the literal beams of wood on which they crucified Christ, but to the whole system of Christian belief, and for the concept of salvation by grace in particular. Similarly, my use of *cross* stands for all that the death of Christ accomplished for those who put their faith in Him.

With the question, "*Can You See the Cross from There?*" I'm asking if you're focusing on the truth and benefits of the gospel, of which the death and resurrection of Jesus serve as the pinnacle. For me, it's easy to focus on myself, on my inadequacies and failures, rather than on what Christ has accomplished for me. I'm also prone to view other people as the primary source of my value and significance, instead of savoring my Savior above all other relationships. In multiple chapters, I'll illustrate my misplaced focus and discuss how to keep the gospel of grace your focal point.

In the book title, *there* refers to any arduous place on your earthly pilgrimage where you're facing off with a threat to your endurance or when you need a fresh, 20-20 view of God's grace as your center of attention.

The Subtitle

The book's subtitle contains two key words: *grace* and *grit*.

Grace is God's lavish love, most vividly demonstrated by His Son's sacrificial death on the cross, where He bore the penalty for sin that we deserve. It's receiving something precious that we don't deserve: His unfathomable, unmerited favor that not only saves us for eternity but also sustains and empowers us so we can grow in holiness and serve Him fruitfully during our earthly pilgrimage.

We most need and appreciate grace when we suffer or sin; when we're broken over our inability to obey God consistently, or when a trial humbles us and instills a desperate dependence on our Savior's enablement.

In this life, no Christian reaches a spiritual plateau high enough to shield himself from the inevitability of sin and from some form of suffering. I'll explain and illustrate the difference our faith in Christ should make in how we respond to either nemesis.

Grit is a person's passionate resolve to keep pursuing a goal or calling despite external challenges and internal weaknesses. It's endurance in the face of difficulties and setbacks. A determination to persist no matter how long and hilly the journey gets. It's perseverance. Stick-to-itiveness. Pluck.

I'm not referring to the bootstrap variety of resilience that one may demonstrate through sheer human willpower. Even within some folks who don't acknowledge God, He has implanted a heroic, surmount-all-obstacles spirit that catapults them to success. But in Christian living and service for Christ, in responding well to sin and to suffering, human resolve isn't enough.

Godly grit relies on the efficacy of faith in the finished work of Christ on the cross. Its origin isn't naturally within us; rather, it consists of determination fueled by the truths and promises embedded within God's Word, which we must appropriate daily. Yes, godly grit requires effort on our part, but it's *grace-motivated effort*, endurance made possible by the flow of divine power into us when we choose to tap into His means of grace.

Chapter Features

Each chapter contains these components:

- A **Faith Poem** in which I pour out my heart on a personal difficulty or issue pertaining to our faith walk.
- **Biblical Reflections** on the subject or need broached in the poem.
- **Prayer Response** is a suggested way to talk to God about the chapter topic.
- **Probes to Ponder** consists of questions to help you personalize and apply what you read.
- **A Pertinent Word** is a Bible text on the theme that supplements verses I may weave into the chapter copy.
- **An Apt Quote** offers another Christian author's reflection on the chapter theme.

Outcome of Your Reading

I write in a popular or conversational style, striving for clarity and practicality, not abstraction. When you finish the book you'll be better prepared to preach to yourself in a biblically informed, cross-exalting manner, as suggested by Paul David Tripp:

> You are constantly preaching to yourself some kind of gospel. You preach to yourself an anti-gospel of your own righteousness, power, and wisdom, or you preach to yourself

the true gospel of deep spiritual need and sufficient grace. You preach to yourself an anti-gospel of aloneness and inability, or you preach to yourself the true gospel of the presence, provision, and power of an ever-present Christ.[1]

I originally intended to produce a one-month devotional book. As I progressed through the writing, the poems, anecdotes and meditations resulted in longer chapters than a typical devotional. But you may still choose to go through the book one chapter a day over a one-month period.

Wherever you are on your faith pilgrimage, I sincerely pray that you maintain a crystal-clear view of the cross and the benefits it offers to Christ-followers.

*What If I'm Not Depressed?

In multiple chapters of this book, I refer to my nemesis of major depression, which I've experienced intermittently since childhood. I illustrate symptoms of depression as well as spiritual practices and divine resources that help me grapple with dark moods. Yet if neither you nor a loved one suffers from depressive episodes, please don't conclude that those chapters aren't relevant to you.

As you read about my ordeal, ask yourself how the biblical truths and spiritual weapons I employ apply to other types of struggles that you face as a Christ-follower. A secondary benefit of describing my bouts with despondency is the enhanced understanding you'll gain of this malady and the greater sensitivity you'll cultivate for persons who experience it.

ONE
CAN YOU SEE THE CROSS CLEARLY?

Eye Trouble

Looming large, within my view,
I pay it the homage due.
I cringe. What an evil glare!
Everywhere I turn, it's there.
Menacing, its taunt is cruel;
an expert at ridicule.
I confess, to find repose.
Louder yet its laugh echoes!
I cannot cut it down to size,
nor hide its features from my eyes.
No matter when or where I look,
I see and feel its jarring hook.

Then God's strong voice breaks through.
He says, "I have a different view.
I can't spot the sin harassing you.
In the way, there is a tree;

two beams crossed at Calvary.
Blood-stained wood is all I see.
Your Substitute: He died and bled.
That's why I see one color: red,
not darkness of your sin instead.
So ever since that cross was built,
I can no longer see your guilt.
Your eyes are prone to deceive.
For better vision, just believe."

———

What Obscures the Cross?

"Eye Trouble" refers to a sin we've confessed which Christ has forgiven, yet remains the subject of Satan's accusations. We feel weighed down by the burden of false guilt despite being forgiven by the Lord. We can't forgive ourselves, as if Jesus' death wasn't sufficient payment for our sin, as if we must add to His sacrifice through our self-condemnation.

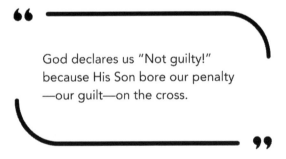

God declares us "Not guilty!" because His Son bore our penalty —our guilt—on the cross.

What is the result? We strive to earn our standing with God instead of reveling in Jesus' performance on our behalf. We may *feel guilty* before God, but if we've put our faith in Christ, we *aren't guilty*!

The second half of the poem alludes to a vital biblical doctrine: *justification*. This aspect of our identity in Christ means that we aren't only forgiven when we put our faith in Christ's death for our sins, but we're also righteous in the eyes of God. Not only are our sins erased when we put faith in Christ, but all of His righteousness—the merit of His sinless life—was credited to us. Now, when God views us, He sees His Son's perfection instead of our sin.

According to Hebrews 10:14, "by one offering He has perfected for all time those who are sanctified" (NASB). Romans 5:1 asserts that we've been justified (declared right before God) through faith in Christ, and the result is, "we have peace with God through our Lord Jesus Christ."

Experientially, sin still plagues us. Confession is still necessary to enjoy heartfelt intimacy with Christ. Positionally, we're right before God. He accepts us based on Jesus' works, never on the basis of how we've performed on any given day. That's why we pray, "In Jesus' name," not in our own name. God declares us "Not guilty!" because His Son bore our penalty— our guilt—on the cross.

Oh God, enable us to grasp and to bask in the benefits of the cross!

Your Position in Christ

To enhance your view of the cross and appropriate its benefits requires a grasp of your status before God. As a Christian, how do you look when viewed through the lens of God's Word?

Picture your salvation as a brilliant, faceted gemstone. View the following aspects of your identity as different facets through which you view your status before God. (Justification is just one of those facets.) There's an overlap among these various aspects of your identity, yet each looks at your salvation from a slightly different angle. The cumulative effect is a greater appreciation for God's saving grace.

Take time to read and meditate on your status as revealed in the following Bible verses.

- *Chosen by God! His initiative in granting you saving grace.* Ephesians 1:3-6
- *Regenerated! (Spiritual rebirth. The work of God's Spirit to instill in you an openness to the gospel that prompted your faith in Christ.)* Titus 3:4-6
- *Justified! Declared right by God!* Romans 5:1, 8-9
- *Forgiven!* Hebrews 10:15-18
- *Unconditionally loved!* Romans 5:6-8; Zephaniah 3:17
- *Not condemned by God!* Romans 8:1
- *Free from the law's demands as a basis for relating to God!* Romans 3:21-22, 28; 8:3-4
- *Purchased by God; Jesus' blood as payment (redemption)!* 1 Corinthians 6:19-20; 1 Peter 1:18-19
- *Secure in Him due to His adoption of you!* John 1:12; Galatians 4:4-6
- *Not guilty! God's wrath toward sin appeased by Jesus' death, satisfying His holiness and justice (propitiation).* 1 John 2:1-2; Romans 3:21-26

- *Peace with God! No longer His enemy; no conflict between you and Him (reconciliation).* Romans 5:10-11; Ephesians 2:1-5

Resources

The following resources thoroughly explore these aspects of your position in Christ. Delve into either book and any fog that obscures your view of the cross will dissipate.

- Robert McGee, *The Search for Significance: Seeing Your True Worth Through God's Eyes*[1]
- Melissa Kruger, Ed., *Identity Theft: Reclaiming the Truth of Who We Are In Christ*[2]

?   Probes to Ponder

To what extent does Satan nag you over past sins that you dealt with before God?

How does the truth of justification help you to counter his accusations?

Though you are positionally perfect before God, why does your day-to-day obedience still matter?

Which aspect of your identity in Christ resonates most with you today? Why? (See the "Your Position in Christ" section.)

If a Christian friend admitted to you that he can't forgive himself for some past sin, how would you verbally respond to him?

Prayer Response

Father, I'm ever so grateful that You can't see my sins since they're covered by Your Son's blood. Oh, what a truth to celebrate and to relish! Don't allow me to take Your forgiveness for granted and use it as an excuse to treat sin lightly. May the reality of the cross compel me to rush into Your presence for confession whenever I blow it, and to seek Your enablement to sin less. In the name of Jesus, the sinless one who died for this sinner, amen.

 A Pertinent Word

For our sake he made him to be sin who knew no sin, so that in him we might become the righteousness of God.

2 Corinthians 5:21

An Apt Quote

I think of the cross as a sponge… a "spiritual sponge" that has taken the sins of mankind—past, present, and future—and absorbed them all. At one awful moment, Christ bore our sins, thus satisfying the righteous demands of the Father, completely and instantaneously clearing up my debt.[3]

—Charles Swindoll, *Growing Deep in the Christian Life*

TWO

WHEN DID JESUS REALLY DIE ON THE CROSS?

Before

Before Christ flailed tiny arms and cried;
before His virgin birth was prophesied,
on a dreaded Roman cross, He died.

Before the star-gazing caravan
took gifts to this infant God-man,
a crown of thorns was the Father's plan.

Before Herod's soldiers would contend;
before the first man and woman sinned,
the Son had decided to condescend.

Before He labeled himself, "I AM!"
Before God spared Isaac with a ram,
Jesus was the sacrificial Lamb.

Before Jesus fought the devil and won;

before Mary conceived the Holy One,
the Father sacrificed His only Son.

Before bread and wine in the upper room;
before His body formed in Mary's womb,
Jesus lay lifeless in a borrowed tomb.

Before Gethsemane's heart-wrenching prayer;
before innkeepers had no room to spare,
Calvary existed. A cross was there!

Some men live without ever knowing why.
Meaning is elusive. They search and they sigh.
Not Jesus Christ. He was born to die.

———

Can a Bible truth both humble us as well as exhilarate us?

Can a concept from God's Word expose our finiteness and cognitive limitations, while simultaneously stirring our soul and prompting worship of God?

Yes, indeed!

In this chapter, I'll share a truth that I can't fully fathom, yet which generates within me sincere gratitude to the Lord. It's an insight that inspired the "Before" poem. This truth focuses on *when* God provided for our salvation and designed a way for sinful people to enjoy intimacy with Him.

When was Jesus really born? When did He die?

Extraordinary Provision

In one sense, God's provision for our salvation, His means of handling the sin problem in a way that would keep intact His holiness and sense of justice, as well as demonstrate His love for His creatures, occurred *long before* New Testament events.

Long before Jesus took His last breath on the cross.

Long before Mary and Joseph cuddled him for the first time in that Bethlehem stable.

Long before the opening of the Old Testament era, when God's plan of redemption began to materialize.

Then when did it happen?

Before Time Began

This particular insight boggles my mind, yet increases my appreciation for God's majesty and infinite wisdom. In 2 Timothy 1:9, the Apostle Paul referred to the power of God that called us to salvation. He called it a salvation "which he gave us in Christ Jesus *before the ages began*" (emphasis mine). The phrase "before the ages began" means "since before time began."

My study led me to Revelation 13:8, a verse that refers to the people whose names are written in the book of life and who will worship Christ in heaven. A common translation of the verse calls Jesus the "Lamb slain *from the foundation of the world*" (emphasis mine, NASB), which refers to a time "before the created order existed."

Imagine: in the inexplicable, mysterious mind of God, He knew that man, the apex of His creation, would sin and need a Savior, someone who would fulfill divine law perfectly and whose righteousness would be applied to us when we put our faith in His sacrificial death. So God designed a way to resolve the enmity between us and Him.

And He did it *when? Before* he created the universe and ultimately populated it with people created in His image. He gave those of us who know Him saving grace long before we needed it! Before there was a garden in Eden where sin entered the human race, in the mind of God there was already a cross on Calvary where His Son would pay its penalty.

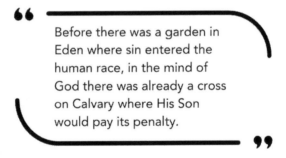

> Before there was a garden in Eden where sin entered the human race, in the mind of God there was already a cross on Calvary where His Son would pay its penalty.

I still can't comprehend it.

I Can't Get Past the When!

Who fully grasps that God provided for our sin problem before He created the earth and human beings? Who comprehends eternity, that God never had a beginning and will never have an end? Indeed, He is, for those of us who put our faith in Christ, "Jehovah-Jireh" (God will provide).

It isn't necessary to fully understand this idea to appreciate it. In fact, if I comprehended God and all His ways...*well, He wouldn't be God!* I'm okay with this mystery. The more I ponder it, the more I worship God.

Meditating on this truth during my devotional times each December helps to counter the inevitable increase in despondency I feel every Christmas season. Though I often don't *feel* the meaning of Christmas, I keep telling myself that the truth doesn't depend on how I feel. Jesus' birth, how He came into the world, why He died and His resurrection are objective historical realities that don't depend on my subjective emotional state for their existence.

Although *why* Jesus was born and died is more important—a purpose which I cite in the last line of the poem—I can't get past the *when* in relation to God's plan of redemption. Nor do I want to get past it. Focusing on God meeting my need for forgiveness *before time began* enhances appreciation for Christ and evokes praise.

? Probes to Ponder

When you contemplate the timing of God's provision for your salvation, what thoughts and feelings well up inside you?

Think of someone you know who needs the encouragement offered by this truth. To explain it to this person, precisely what would you say? When will you carve out an opportunity to share it?

Prayer Response

Oh Father, thank You for this reassuring truth about the timing of Your plan to save me. What a need-meeting God—meeting my need for a Savior even before creation! Nonetheless, keep reminding me of when Jesus' incarnation actually took place and enable me to see the cross and its benefits clearly. I especially need to remember this on those days when sadness tries to eclipse the Son and His cross from my view. In the name of Jesus, the Light of the World who continues to penetrate my darkness, amen.

A Pertinent Word

Blessed be the God and Father of our Lord Jesus Christ, who has blessed us in Christ with every spiritual blessing in the heavenly places, even as he chose us in him before the foundation of the world, that we should be holy and blameless before him.

Ephesians 1:3-4

❞ An Apt Quote

On the cross, the Father would forsake the Son and pour out all his wrath upon him. We cannot imagine the horror and stripping felt by the God-man Jesus Christ when his Father poured out wrath on him and forsook him. Jesus was forsaken so that we would have the assurance that we never will be.[1]

—Elyse Fitzpatrick, *Comforts from the Cross*

THREE

HOW ARE YOU FILLING THAT GOD-SHAPED VOID?

Satisfy Me

I have needs that no one can fill.
Not wife nor kids nor friends can heal
the deepest hurts, the yearning for
a perfect love, for something more.
Then who will hear and heed this cry?
Just You, oh God, can satisfy.
So fill the void, the empty space,
within my heart with Your own face.

Yes, feed this hungry heart of mine
until You are its Valentine;
until my heart has cast aside
the things on which I have relied;
until we know close fellowship
and I hold You with tighter grip.
Until my restlessness is gone,
and I'm consumed with You alone.

———

What generated the poem was a niggling awareness that none of God's blessings I've received—a loving family; priceless friendships; a challenging ministry platform and sufficient material provision—meet my deepest personal need: *intimacy with Jesus Christ.*

Unrealistic Expectations

I tend to put too much stock in human relationships, setting unrealistic expectations for others. Also, I've occasionally over-worked, all the while neglecting high-priority relationships, including unhurried time with the Lord, for whom I was burning out. The wrong places in which I've sought happiness, identity and fulfillment haven't typically been areas of sin; rather, they've been good and necessary things (or people) that I've idolized.

Whether our pursuit of fulfillment includes illicit relationships, rampant accumulation of wealth, public name recognition, or a skewed reliance on good and necessary things, there's still a God-shaped vacuum within us that only intimacy with God fulfills.

Here's how C.S. Lewis put it:

> God wants to be our perfect lover, but instead we seek perfection in human relationships and are disappointed when our lovers cannot love us perfectly. God wants to provide our ultimate security, but we seek our safety in power and possessions and then find we must continually

worry about them. We seek satisfaction of our spiritual longing in a host of ways that may have very little to do with God.[1]

Augustine echoed the sentiment that only God can satisfy our deepest longings: "You have made us for yourself, O Lord, and our hearts are restless until they rest in you."[2]

Investment in key human relationships and focusing on our relationship with God do not constitute an either/or proposition. God often loves and nurtures us through other people He brings into our lives. We neglect either sphere of relationship, vertical or horizontal, to our detriment. But this is what I've learned: excessive reliance on other people, while neglecting intimacy with the Lord, won't fill the God-shaped void within us. That's especially true when we're relying on others, instead of God, to fill our deepest need for security and belonging.

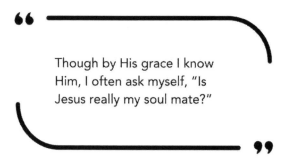

> Though by His grace I know Him, I often ask myself, "Is Jesus really my soul mate?"

Though by His grace I know Him, I often ask myself, "Is Jesus really my *soul mate*?"

Is He yours?

A Realistic Perspective

There's a sense in which even a close relationship with God can't fully satisfy us in this life. This isn't due to a fault in God, but in us. Here, sin still dogs us and hinders our enjoyment of God. Only when we see our Lord face to face will we be like Him and worship Him without hindrances.

Even in a godly person who's walking with Christ daily, whose priorities are in order, a deep hunger or yearning may persist —an almost indefinable longing for more.

Can you relate?

I think of this perspective when I hear or read another one of C.S. Lewis' well-known remarks: "If I find in myself a desire which no experience in this world can satisfy, the most probable explanation is that I was made for another world."[3]

Only in heaven will this subtle longing for something more be satisfied. Though our intimacy with Christ won't reach its zenith in this life, pursuing a measure of intimacy with Him *now* will at least fill more of that inner void than any other relationship or thing.

?   Probes to Ponder

To what extent are you relying too much on earthly relationships, possessions or circumstances for your meaning and identity?

What is the inevitable consequence of expecting too much from other people, things or circumstances?

How is it possible to appreciate and enjoy God's gifts without substituting them for Him?

How are you currently cultivating intimacy with Him?

 Prayer Response

Father, like any other relationship, cultivating intimacy with You takes time and grace-motivated effort. Every time I think I'm too busy to spend unhurried time with You, remind me of the benefits of nurturing my relationship with You. If Jesus felt the need to pray to You often while on earth, oh, how much more I need it! I ask this in Your Son's name, who always did the things that were pleasing to You, amen.

 A Pertinent Word

And this is eternal life, that they know you, the only true God, and Jesus Christ whom you have sent.

John 17:3

 An Apt Quote

Sin causes us to look horizontally for what can only be found vertically. Creation was never designed to satisfy your heart. Creation was made to be a big finger pointing you to the One who alone has the ability to satisfy your heart. We seek horizontally for the personal rest that we are to find vertically, and it never works. Looking to others for your inner sense of well-being is pointless. The people around you aren't typically interested in taking on the burden of being your personal messiah. They don't want to live with the responsibility of having your identity in their hands. Looking to people for your inner self-worth never works. That's why the reality that Jesus has become your righteousness is so precious. His grace has forever freed us from needing to prove our righteousness and our worth.[4]

—Paul Tripp, *New Morning Mercies*

FOUR
ARE YOU OVERLOADED AND STRESSED?

Divine Curriculum

I often don't see rhyme or reason
for the things that come my way.
Sometimes the pressure intensifies
and I'm too confused to pray.

Sometimes God nurtures with darkness,
and my soul aches for more light.
Or I arrive at my rope's end;
extreme weakness is my plight.

Sometimes God answers with silence,
and waiting on Him is His will.
Sometimes I can't see the finish line;
the race seems too long and uphill.

But would living require any faith
if I understood all of God's ways?

Tuition seems steep for God's teaching,
yet in the long run, each lesson pays.

I learned to rely not on self, but on God.
I need His Spirit's filling every day;
to hold Him close, to feed on His Word.
Only then I have something to say.

———

A period of prayerful reflection after my first year of teaching at Columbia Bible College (now Columbia International University) inspired this poem. Perhaps the most time-consuming, pressure-packed, energy-draining year for a college professor is the first one. Every course and each day's lesson plans were first-time originals for me, demanding hours of fresh study and brainstorming.

Engulfed by Exhaustion

By the end of that 1981-82 school year, fatigue of mind, body and spirit overwhelmed me. My body protested lack of sleep. My mind desperately needed a pause in the process of producing. I had pressed down so hard on the accelerator for nine months that my internal engine broke down. I was out of fuel and numerous inner parts needed to be replaced or rebuilt.

"Burnout" was an apt descriptor for my condition. A nine-month adrenalin rush left me reeling. Despite favorable student ratings, unhappiness and restlessness seized me. I had committed to teaching a summer course but told the dean I didn't have the mental and physical reserves left to teach it. I constantly felt anxious, overreacting emotionally to the normal stressors of life. A dark, melancholy mood enveloped me.

Spiritual dryness set in as well. During the school year I had set aside time for prayer and devotional Bible reading, but I often hurried through those quiet times. The incessant demands of each day's tasks clamored for my attention. I lost a sense of the Lord's presence by the end of the school year. Motivation to pray, teach or write waned.

Puzzled, I wondered if God had abandoned me. Was I smack-dab in the middle of a spiritual crisis? Had my faith faltered? Why did I feel so empty? My soul felt like the cracked, parched earth on the floor of a desert.

My condition prompted me to reserve time to analyze my first-year experience. For a part of several days, I delved into God's Word, prayed earnestly and journaled. I asked the Lord to show me how to prevent this from happening again. I identified three lessons that you'll find applicable as well.

Lesson # 1: The Body's Debt Collection

God's Spirit pointed out that I rarely took a full day off over those nine months. Most weeks I took my wife on a date. I often played with my two young boys, and I tucked them into bed and prayed with them every evening. Though I didn't significantly neglect my family, I still worked half a day many Saturdays. And despite the college's prohibition against class-related tasks on Sundays, I often worked an hour or two that day as well. I didn't give my mind, body and spirit their desperately needed rest. I realize that vocational ministry isn't a nine-to-five, 40-hour-a-week job, yet I went overboard in my zeal for the Lord's work.

I neglected the Lord's "Sabbath principle" to my own peril. Refusing to take a full day off each week was tantamount to telling God that I was indispensable to Him, that He couldn't accomplish as much without my constant effort—an absurd and heretical thought!

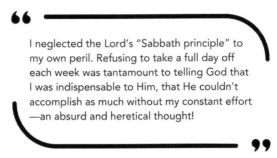

> I neglected the Lord's "Sabbath principle" to my own peril. Refusing to take a full day off each week was tantamount to telling God that I was indispensable to Him, that He couldn't accomplish as much without my constant effort —an absurd and heretical thought!

Here's what I learned from that year's ministry overload: *an intense expenditure of energy over time depletes one's physical, mental and emotional reserves.*

Your energy depletion or spiritual dryness may happen after you take a short-term mission trip overseas that involves a lot of teaching. After you plan and implement a weekend retreat for a target group in your church. After you finish an advanced degree while still working full time. After completing a project for your company that requires consistent overtime for several weeks. After months of caregiving for a sick or disabled loved one.

The typical effect on Christ-followers of such concentrated output is a period of dryness that numbs us to the Lord's presence and drains motivation for normal responsibilities and activities. My melancholy, sensitive temperament exacerbated these symptoms, but the phenomenon can happen to anyone after a protracted, earnest time of output.

I recall a story, occurring over a century ago in Africa, of natives who worked as porters for missionaries. Their trip on foot took several days. The missionaries, eager to reach their destination, pushed the porters harder on the third day. On the fourth day, after a much shorter distance, the natives stopped, refusing to go any farther.

Their explanation? "We went so quickly yesterday that we must wait for our souls to catch up with us!"[1]

No, that summer in 1982 I wasn't victimized by a spiritual crisis. My faith hadn't failed. God had not withdrawn His presence. God's "divine curriculum" in the form of burnout taught me this lesson:

The human body always collects its debts!

The next time you engage in an intense period of ministry or other work-related output, give yourself permission not to feel much for a while. Don't make any important decisions until you feel replenished. Tell yourself it's okay to sleep in or take a nap. To play more. To take long walks. To read a book for pleasure, not because it's required for your work.

Exercise patience: your normal zest for the Lord, for life and ministry, will return after some down time. Heed the counsel of prolific author and missionary Elisabeth Elliot: "Rest is a weapon given to us by God. The enemy hates it because he wants you stressed and occupied."[2]

What happens if you don't rest and replenish your energy in some form? Your vulnerability to temptation will escalate and your irritability will mushroom. You'll discover that your soul hasn't caught up to your body's frantic pace.

Lesson #2: Input and Output

The energy and creativity needed for ministry tasks stem from input I receive from unhurried times with the Lord, especially through His Word and prayer. I accomplish less when I neglect Him because I'm relying on human resources and reserves separated from His work within me. That first year on the faculty, my service, to some extent, eclipsed my seeking Him, rather than my seeking of the Lord fueling my service.

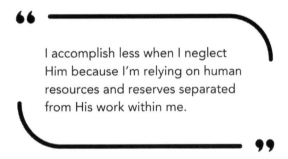

> I accomplish less when I neglect Him because I'm relying on human resources and reserves separated from His work within me.

In Colossians 1:28-29, Paul wrote:

> Him we proclaim, warning everyone and teaching everyone with all wisdom that we may present everyone mature in

Christ. For this I toil, *struggling with all his energy that he powerfully works within me* (emphasis mine).

Paul utilized a strong Greek word, translated *struggling*. It refers to tenacious, difficult labor tantamount to wrestling. He implied that his evangelism and discipling ministries consisted of hard work and long hours. How did Paul keep going and avoid burnout? He emphasized that divine input fueled his capacity for significant output. His secret was Christ's energy working in and through him.

Though imperfectly applied, since that first year on the faculty, I've kept in the forefront of my mind what Ron Dunn called, "Paul's definition of ministry," which he gleaned from Colossians 1:28-29. *"Ministry is my putting out whatever the Lord is putting into me."* [3]

Lesson #3: Joy Stealers

Psalm 100:1-2 states, "Make a joyful noise to the Lord, all the earth! *Serve the Lord with gladness!* Come into his presence with singing" (emphasis mine). Due to my experience of exhaustion in 1982, whenever ministry becomes drudgery and joyless, I enter the Lord's presence and ask Him these hard questions.

- What is stealing the joy of serving You? Is my life imbalanced?
- What sources of spiritual, physical and mental energy am I neglecting?
- Am I accepting too many ministry opportunities outside of my required responsibilities?

- Am I accepting discretionary duties that don't mesh with my grace-gifts?
- Am I tolerating sin in an area of my life for which I need to confess?

Poetic Reflection

Why did I title the poem, "Divine Curriculum"?

The term "curriculum" stems from the concept of a *racecourse*. Figuratively speaking, applied to schools such as the Christian university where I served, curriculum refers to the racecourse students run through in order to reach the finish line (graduation). That racecourse includes both required courses and experiences, as well as optional opportunities for growth and development.

Divine curriculum refers to the racecourse God sovereignly designs for each of His children: the events, experiences and people He brings into our lives to develop our character and to increase our usefulness to Him. It even includes difficulties caused by our unwise choices (such as my imbalanced schedule), which He redeems for our good and His glory.

When we cry out to Him as pressure mounts, the Lord takes the challenging situation and employs it to deepen our character and to prompt ever-increasing dependency on Him. That's the perspective offered in the final stanza of the "Divine Curriculum" poem.

Resources

If this chapter whets your appetite for resources that speak to the issue of burnout and skewed priorities, examine these books:

Mark Buchanan, *The Rest of God: Restoring Your Soul by Restoring Sabbath*[4]

John Ortberg, *Soul Keeping: Caring for the Most Important Part of You*[5]

Richard Swenson, *Margin: Restoring Emotional, Physical, Financial and Time Reserves to Our Overloaded Lives*[6]

Charles Hummel, *Tyranny of the Urgent*[7]

Gordon MacDonald, *Ordering Your Private World* (Revised and Updated Edition)[8]

? Probes to Ponder

Why do we struggle to achieve more balance or margin in our schedules? Is our identity rooted in what we do for Christ rather than in what He did for us on the cross?

Can you identify a stressful "course" or time in your life when God tested or stretched your faith? In retrospect, do you see a positive outcome? Did this difficult part of the racecourse God designed for you magnify His glory in some manner, either in your eyes or in the eyes of persons who know you? Have you thanked Him for assigning that course to you?

Whether you serve the Lord vocationally or as a volunteer, Ron Dunn's definition of ministry pertains to you: "*Ministry is my putting out what the Lord is putting into me.*" Do you need to make any adjustments in your schedule, so the Lord has ample opportunity to fuel your work with the energy that only He provides?

Review the evaluative questions in the "Joy Stealers" section of this chapter. At this particular time in your life, do you need to ask Him those questions?

Prayer Response

Heavenly Father, when I'm prone to accept too many responsibilities, overwork and neglect my Sabbath rest, remind me first, that my drive to "produce" for You reveals a lack of faith in You. Subtly, I'm assuming that You can't manage things without me—a preposterous idea! Remind me that You will exist after I die and that cemeteries are filled with indispensable people. And, my drivenness indicates that I'm basing my identity and my sense of significance on what I do, not on what You did for me through Christ's death. Help me to serve out of gratitude for what Your Son accomplished for me, not in an attempt to prove my value. In the name of Jesus, who, after His disciples returned from a ministry mission, said to them, "Come away by yourselves to a desolate place and rest a while" (Mark 6:31), amen.

A Pertinent Word

Be still, and know that I am God. I will be exalted among the nations; I will be exalted in the earth!

Psalm 46:10

66,99 An Apt Quote

We must have some room to breathe. We need freedom to think and permission to heal. Our relationships are being starved to death by velocity. No one has the time to listen, let alone to love. Our children lay wounded on the ground, run over by our high-speed good intentions. Is God now pro-exhaustion? Doesn't He lead people beside the still waters anymore? Who plundered these wide-open spaces of the past and how can we get them back? There are no fallow lands for our emotions to lie down and rest in.[9]

—Richard Swenson, *Margin*

FIVE
DO YOU WANT TO STAY THE SAME?

Don't Let Me Stay the Same

Please do not let me stay the same.
I'll bring more glory to Your name
if transformation is the norm.
Chisel away until You form
in me the image of Your Son,
and I'm no longer on the run
from Your Spirit, who pursues me
so He can revive and use me.

I want no way of pain ignored,
so truthfully, I'll call you "Lord."
Please judge the contents of my mind.
Turn up the heat, so I'm refined
and rebel thoughts that once held sway
are clamped in chains and led away.
Throughout my heart beam Spirit's light
until impurities take flight;

until my sin produces tears
and vision blocked by Satan clears.

Your pruning work will hurt, I know,
but You must cut for fruit to grow.
Replace anxiety with peace.
Remove my restlessness. Increase
my confidence that You control
my circumstances, that Your goal
in all that happens is my joy.
Whatever means that You employ
to change me will be worth the price:
investment, not a sacrifice.

When I'm at home upon my knees,
You'll be the One I yearn to please.
Keep breaking me until I'm tame;
just do not let me stay the same.

————

Process of Spiritual Transformation

Do you ever feel frustrated by the slow, inconsistent nature of spiritual growth?

Three steps forward, two steps back.

That's a realistic depiction of spiritual formation. At best, it's a zigzagging line on a graph, showing highs and lows. Over time, though, the line charting the progress should reveal a higher plateau when compared to the starting point at our conversion. Even with setbacks, we should be a step ahead of where we were. As Bill Jones put it, "As we grow, we won't be sinless, yet we should sin less."[1]

One catalyst for change is prayer, which acknowledges the need for the Holy Spirit to shape us more into the image of Christ. The poem is a prayer that captures my heart's plea for ongoing change and growth.

Growth is both a human and divine endeavor. Our responsibility is choosing to use the "means of grace" God has provided: prayer, Bible study, corporate worship, service and need-meeting fellowship with other believers, just to name a few. God has chosen to work supernaturally through these means of grace to transform our hearts and minds, so we grow in Christlikeness. What we choose to do merely puts us in a position for God to transform us. What we do is "sow to the Spirit" (Galatians 6:8). Then His Spirit starts changing us from the inside-out.

In his book *Spiritual Rhythm,* Mark Buchanan refers to our part in the transformation God wants to work in us:

> Personal renewal requires the establishment of spiritual practices, what I call holy habits. But what starts spontaneously must be sustained deliberately. It's the time for resolve, a clear and firm decisiveness about what matters. For now, you will live this way, not that. From now on, you will go in this direction, not that. And with this resolve, you then reorder your life—how you give, pray, read, serve, and think —to both nurture and reflect your resolve.[2]

Even if our part is just crying out to the Lord with a heartfelt yearning to change, like I did through the poem, that's a good start!

Poem lyrics also suggest that personal change may involve difficulty or pain. I use images of refining (Job 23:10) and pruning (John 15:2) to emphasize the uncomfortable process required to make us more godly and fruitful. Like a blacksmith reshaping or creating an object with fire and hammer, positive change may require painful blows.

Yet staying the same may hurt more.

An Encouraging Perspective

I compare the slow, arduous process of my own spiritual growth to the speed of a snail covered in molasses. That's when God's Spirit uses this truth to encourage me: *I am not yet the person I want to be, but thanks to God's grace, I'm not who I once was, either!*

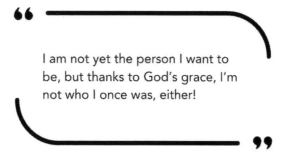

I am not yet the person I want to be, but thanks to God's grace, I'm not who I once was, either!

❓ Probes to Ponder

To what extent is your desire in harmony with the words of the poem? Are you willing to pray those lyrics to the Lord as your plea for personal transformation?

Look back over your pilgrimage as a Christian. When you experienced a season of noticeable spiritual growth, what were the catalysts for change?

Can you identify a time when a trial or setback provided the impetus for spiritual growth? Have you thanked the Lord for redeeming that pain for your good and His glory?

In what area of your life is the Holy Spirit currently prompting you to change? What can you do to cooperate with Him in this process, to put yourself in a place where He will empower you?

🙏 Prayer Response

O Lord, for Your Spirit to accomplish transformation within me, what is my responsibility? What choices must I make, what must I do differently, to put myself in a place to receive Your enablement? Remind me daily that though change is a supernatural work of Your Spirit, not merely a human endeavor, I must choose to use the means of grace You provide and through which You choose to work. In the name of Jesus, the only man who ever lived who didn't need to grow spiritually, amen.

A Pertinent Word

And we all, with unveiled face, beholding the glory of the Lord, are being transformed into the same image from one degree of glory to another. For this comes from the Lord who is the Spirit.

2 Corinthians 3:18

 ## An Apt Quote

The following excerpt from Elyse Fitzpatrick's devotional book, *Comforts from the Cross,* cites the primary prerequisite for spiritual growth and greater obedience to the Lord. Though I've emphasized our responsibility to use means of God's grace, she wisely cites where our primary focus should be in our pursuit of holiness. She urges us to cultivate more consistent obedience by keeping our eyes not on ourselves, but on the love of God, as demonstrated by His Son's sacrificial death on the cross for us. Without applying this perspective, we won't choose to use God's means of grace.

> If love for God isn't present in our heart, then Godward obedience will be absent in our life. The key to a godly life is not more and more self-generated effort. Jesus said, in effect, that if we love Him, your obedience will flow naturally from that love. The secret to obedience isn't formulaic steps found in a self-help book. It is a relentless pursuit of love for him.
>
> How then do I cultivate the sincerity of love that motivates obedience? By focusing more intently on his love for me

than on my love for him, more on his obedience than on mine, more on his faithfulness than mine, more on his strength than mine. The plain truth is that my love for God (and hence, my obedience) will grow as I cultivate my comprehension of his vast love for me. If we neglect this key by focusing too narrowly on ourselves, our success or failure, then we'll become mired down in guilt or pride, neither of which will stimulate loving obedience. Resting in the awareness of our perfect acceptance before Him and in his intense desire to have us for his own will cause us to want to please him.[3]

SIX

CAN YOU THANK GOD FOR PAIN?

Thank You for the Pain

Thank You for the broken heart;
it is softer than before.
Since the pain ripped it apart,
it's insensitive no more.
How can I accept the pain?
Now I am more prone to pray,
to yield to Your mighty reign
and to let You have Your way.

I've no choice but to depend
upon Your sustaining grace.
You will pay a dividend
for each tear upon my face.
For You accept as sacrifice
a heart that's broken in two.
You already paid the price
for the pain I'm going through.

There is no way I would choose
this hurt, all the times I've cried.
Yet it's a gift I won't refuse,
for it cleanses me inside.
I'm driven to wield Your Sword;
to give Your Spirit His due.
So thank You for the pain, Lord,
for it draws me close to You.

———

That's a poem I wrote while in the throes of a depressive episode. Neither prayer nor medical intervention and counseling removed the despondency, so I figured God wanted to use it redemptively. His Spirit reminded me of how desperately I cling to Him during such times, which is a good thing. The lyrics cite these benefits of my despondent spirit: increased dependence on and intimacy with the Lord; a softer heart; a hunger for God's Word; prayer for sustenance and inner cleansing.

Grateful for Despondency

Any type of trial potentially offers benefits. My depression is merely a case in point. How the nemesis of despondency contributes to my spiritual development can also become true for you in relation to your own trials.

When despair generates bouts of weeping, my heart is softer than usual. It's during such times that the Holy Spirit often convicts me of wrong thoughts or behavior patterns. Since I'm already in a dependent state due to depression, I pray more often, if only for relief. And anytime I'm in a "seeking God" mode, the Holy Spirit is more liable to engage in a purifying work within my heart. In a sense, tears serve as a cleansing agent for me. Anything that softens my heart makes me more receptive to the Holy Spirit and what He wants to do in my heart.

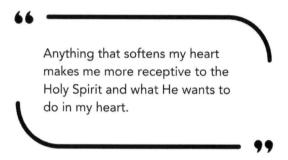

Anything that softens my heart makes me more receptive to the Holy Spirit and what He wants to do in my heart.

Discouragement drives me to the Word of God for relief. Memorization of promises, especially from the Psalms and Prophetic books, instills a disciplined study habit that carries over long after a dark mood lifts. I'm reminded of the hard truth in Psalm 119:71, that suffering of any sort deepens my dependence on God's Word: "It is good for me that I was afflicted, that I might learn Your statutes."

Paul illustrated this perspective. His burdensome experience of persecution wielded benefits for the spiritual realm. Referring to an affliction he encountered in Asia, he wrote: "For we were so utterly burdened beyond our strength that we despaired of life itself. Indeed, we felt that we had received the sentence of death. But that was to make us rely not on ourselves but on God who raises the dead" (2 Corinthians 1:8-9).

Like Paul, pain and adverse circumstances of any kind inevitably draw me closer to the Lord. That's why I thanked Him for the pain in poetic form.

? Probes to Ponder

Can you identify a time when God used a painful experience to facilitate a time of spiritual renewal? How should that remembrance affect your attitude toward a current stressor?

How is having "nowhere to look but up" a good thing?

Identify a current challenge or adversity. Are you willing to say this to the Lord? "Lord, please don't waste this pain! Redeem it somehow, for my good and for Your glory."

🙏 Prayer Response

Allow the words of my prayer to serve as a catalyst for what you need to say to God concerning your own source of affliction. Just as I cite my despondency in the prayer, your adaptation should pinpoint a current personal challenge.

Father, I don't enjoy hard times, whether they're due to challenging circumstances or to temperamental weaknesses. Yet so far, the special graces of prayer and Your Word have not removed my depression, nor have the common graces of medicine or counseling eradicated it. Though I'll keep fighting for my joy, I do recognize that this form of affliction has kept me desperately dependent on You, and that's a good thing. Thank You for using my pain this way. In the name of Jesus, "who for the joy

that was set before him endured the cross" (Hebrews 12:2),
amen.

 ## A Pertinent Word

Therefore, since we have been justified by faith, we have peace
with God through our Lord Jesus Christ. Through him we
have also obtained access by faith into this grace in which we
stand, and we rejoice in hope of the glory of God. Not only
that, but we rejoice in our sufferings, knowing that suffering
produces endurance, and endurance produces character, and
character produces hope, and hope does not put us to shame,
because God's love has been poured into our hearts through
the Holy Spirit who has been given to us.

Romans 5:1-5

 ## An Apt Quote

Joni Eareckson Tada, who has been a quadriplegic since a
diving accident in her teens, gave this testimony:

> Somehow, in the midst of your own suffering, the Son of
> God beckons you into the inner sanctum of His own
> suffering—a place of mystery and privilege. I have suffered,
> yes. But I wouldn't trade places with anybody in the world
> to be this close to Jesus.[1]

> God, thank You for the deeper healing You gave me. That
> no (for physical healing) meant yes to a stronger faith in
> You, a deeper prayer life, and a greater understanding of

Your Word. It has purged sin from my life, forced me to depend on Your grace, and increased my compassion for others who hurt. It has stirred an excitement about heaven and pushed me to give thanks in times of sorrow. It has helped me to love You more, Jesus.[2]

—*Beside Bethesda: 31 Days Toward Deeper Healing*

SEVEN

HOW IS SUFFERING A DIVINE GRACE?

Like Falling Rain

My tears descend like falling rain.
Their constant flow reveals the pain
of much regret, of fragile heart.
I cannot stop them once they start.

With each teardrop there is an ache.
I did not know one's heart could break
so many times in just one day.
Despondency won't go away.

I shout! Yet God seems not to hear.
He leaves untouched my hurt, my fear.
Where is the God of Abraham?
Where's El Shaddai, the great "I AM?"

Like falling rain, despair descends.
Are there not any dividends

to faith within the here and now?
Will God assist me? When? And how?

Does He not care when what I feel
makes dying grow in its appeal?
Though it's racked by doubt, my mind turns
to God's Word. Here is what it learns.

He gave His Spirit. He is near!
In time He'll wipe away each tear.
Though I do not know how or when,
my lips will smile and sing again.

Christ understands the tears I've shed.
He also wept before He bled.
His cross absorbed His tears and mine.
Heart-rending pain serves to refine.

God never acts except from love.
My darkness was designed above
for fruitfulness, and for my gain.
It's grace outpoured, like falling rain!

———

The depression in my spirit mimicked the weather that autumn morning: dark, low-lying clouds; wind-whipped brown leaves flying several feet off the ground and uninterrupted falling rain.

A heavy sadness inside me spawned a flow of tears almost as constant as the rainfall. The heartache was relentless: an emotional ache analogous to the throbbing of a raw wound on the body where the flesh beneath the skin is exposed.

Choosing to Focus on God's Word

As often is the case, I wasn't sure why I felt so gloomy that day. I can't always identify a reason for the arrival of a depressive episode. Yet as I struggled through the day, an intentional decision to focus on God's Word offered perspective, the capacity to view my pain through the eyes of an all-loving, in-control God. The poem cites my heaviness of spirit as well as the following truths from God's Word that enabled me to fight back against the despair vying for control of my mind.

Apply these insights to whatever affliction you currently face:

- *God is sovereign.* Nothing can happen to me without His permission. As David put it, "My times are in Your hand" (Psalm 31:15a).
- *I remembered Romans 8:28*: "And we know that for those who love God all things work together for good, for those who are called according to his purpose." (I also thought of Romans 8:29, which mentions the goal of Christlikeness for His followers. I figured the "all things" in verse 28 are prerequisites for cultivating the image of Jesus within me.)
- *I meditated on Jesus' own experience in the Garden of Gethsemane, where distress prior to His arrest overwhelmed Him.* According to Mark 14:33-35, He felt "greatly distressed and troubled." His soul was "very sorrowful, even to death." Hebrews 5:7 asserts, "In the days of his flesh, Jesus offered up prayers and

supplications, with loud cries and tears, to him who was able to save him from death, and he was heard because of his reverence." Meditating on the fact that Jesus understood my painful human emotions and identified with my humanity prompted me to cry out to Him off and on that dreary day. I felt encouraged because I realized that the cross is the ultimate example of how God redeems pain!

- *The words of Psalm 30:5 sustained me*: "Weeping may tarry for the night, but joy comes with the morning."
- *Based on Revelation 21:4, I fixed my hope on the promise of the new heaven and the new earth*: "He will wipe away every tear from their eyes, and death shall be no more, neither shall there be mourning, nor crying, nor pain anymore." As I camped out on that verse, God's Spirit whispered, "Terry, don't give up! Your weaknesses of body and temperament are temporary. Depression won't always harass you!"

As I fought against despair that day, I didn't feel like a winner. Yet God's Word buoyed my spirit time and again against the huge waves of despondency, enabling me to carry on with my ministry of teaching without throwing in the towel.

> I felt encouraged because I realized that the cross is the ultimate example of how God redeems pain!

❓ Probes to Ponder

When has truth from God's Word sustained you through a hardship?

What comforting truth or verses does the Holy Spirit bring to your mind right now?

Which of the insights from God's Word that sustained me resonates most with you today?

Who in your sphere of influence could benefit from your story, and from the verses that instilled hope within you during a time of discouragement?

🙏 Prayer Response

Father, thank You that for every color of trial I go through, You meet me with a corresponding color of grace! I'm grateful, Jesus, that You don't chide me when I'm melancholy; rather, You welcome me with open arms and say, "Come to Me, all who labor and are heavy laden, and I will give you rest" (Matthew 11:28). And Holy Spirit, I appreciate the way You remind me of Bible verses that You inspired just when I need them. In the name of the Savior, who also experienced emotional pain and prayed with loud crying and tears, amen.

A Pertinent Word

For we do not have a high priest who is unable to sympathize with our weaknesses, but one who in every respect has been tempted as we are, yet without sin. Let us then with confidence draw near to the throne of grace, that we may receive mercy and find grace to help in time of need.

Hebrews 4:15-16

,,   An Apt Quote

Bodily pain should help us understand the cross, but mental depression should make us apt scholars of Gethsemane. The sympathy of Jesus is the next most precious thing to his sacrifice. To feel in our being that God to whom we cry has himself suffered as we do enables us to feel that we are not alone and that God is not cruel.[1]

—Charles Spurgeon, as quoted in Zack Eswine's *Spurgeon's Sorrows*

EIGHT
DO YOU NOTICE GOD'S MASTERPIECES?

Living That Makes Sense

Soak up the sunrise.
Work will wait. Absorb the Lord's art.
Let eye-popping hues heat up your heart.

Crunch the crisp apple.
Relish its juice running down your chin
before you choose to bite it again.

Ball up the blowing snow.
Let red-cold fingers form snowmen;
frosty flakes melt on face's skin.

Listen! Don't just hear
when brown leaves scrunch beneath your shoe
or contented cats purr on cue.

Life is a sponge. Fill it, then seize it.

With all your might, twist it and squeeze it.

———

Engaging with Creation

Engaging with nature offers mental and physical health benefits for almost everyone. Fresh air, sunshine, beauty and exercise work in tandem to lower stress and refresh the spirit. Many folks say their capacity to think through solutions to problems escalates when they're taking a walk outdoors.

For people dealing with a desolate spirit, engaging with nature often serves as potent medicine. A case in point for me occurred on the way to work when a roseate sunrise greeted me and displayed the creative majesty of God. That moment of ravishing beauty made a depressive episode more bearable. The splendid view reminded me of Psalm 8:1: "O Lord, our Lord, how majestic is your name in all the earth! You have set your glory above the heavens."

That fleeting example of God's artistry inflated my spirit and offered more than enough zest to fill the demands of that day with more than usual cheerfulness. When I gazed at the sunrise, I recalled a popular saying: "Life is not a dress rehearsal. Live it to the fullest."

That morning, I lived life to the fullest by staring at the sunrise. Later that day, I penned the poem.

Probes to Ponder

Think of a time when you observed extraordinary beauty in nature. Where were you? What did you see? How did the view affect your concept of or feelings about God, our Creator? Did you thank Him for what you observed?

What benefits have you reaped from spending time outdoors?

What outdoor places have you intended to visit, yet so far, those places remain stuck in the realm of good intentions?

 Prayer Response

Father, may I never take for granted the joy-instilling, stress-relieving benefits of observing Your artistry in creation. The universe is Your canvas. Your palette offers colors I couldn't imagine in a score of lifetimes. I never knew how well purple goes with orange and pink until I stared at that sunrise! What I viewed revealed Your majesty, reminding me that You are more than capable of meeting my needs and handling my problems. In the name of Your Son, who, along with the Holy Spirit, was with You at the time of creation, amen.

A Pertinent Word

The heavens declare the glory of God, and the sky above proclaims his handiwork.

Psalm 19:1

💬 An Apt Quote

I like to see my Savior on the hills and by the shores of the sea. I hear my Father's voice in the thunder and listen to the whispers of His love in the cadence of the sunlit waves. These are my Father's works. I admire them and I seem all the nearer to Him when I am among them. If I were a great artist, I would think it a very small compliment if my son came into my house and said he would not notice the pictures I had painted because he only wanted to think of *me*. He therein would condemn my paintings, for if they were good for anything, he would be rejoiced to see my hand in them! Oh, but surely, everything that comes from the hand of such a Master Artist as God has something in it of Himself! The Lord rejoices in His works and shall not His people do so?[1]

—Charles Spurgeon

NINE
IS THAT A THERMOMETER IN YOUR MOUTH?

Words from the Heart

My words aren't always soft or sweet.
I've said things labeled indiscreet.
When I'm not Spirit-filled I'm prone
to couch my words in toxic tone.

With feelings worn upon my sleeve
come words I wish I could retrieve.
I regret times that I've been caught
speaking without engaging thought.

I must not underestimate
how deeply my words penetrate.
Everything a person hears
goes to the heart, not just the ears.

Let my words give comfort and grace
and put a smile upon the face

of all who hear the things I say.
Let my words help, not hurt, I pray.

Yes, I must guard my wayward heart,
for that is where the wrong words start.
The problem is not with my speech.
It's putting God far out of reach.

It's prayerlessness. I can't afford
to rely on self and not the Lord.
My tongue is far too wild to tame
unless God's glory is my aim.

———

Vital Sign of Health

When a young child acts cranky or listless, a parent pops a thermometer into the kid's mouth or scans the child's forehead with a device that reveals the body's temperature. If the temp is much above 98.6 degrees, the mother or father knows there's an infection on the inside that needs medical attention. No matter why we visit the doctor's office, a nurse usually takes our temperature. That's because body temperature is a vital sign of physical health. A reading above the norm signals trouble somewhere in the body and prompts the doctor to diagnose the illness.

Similarly, *the tongue is a vital sign of spiritual health.*

Our speech patterns provide a good indicator of the condition of our hearts. Our conversations show whether there's an infection in the heart that needs immediate attention. Here's how Jesus put it: "The good person out of the good treasure of his heart produces good, and the evil person out of his evil treasure produces evil, *for out of the abundance of the heart his mouth speaks*" (Luke 6:45, emphasis mine).

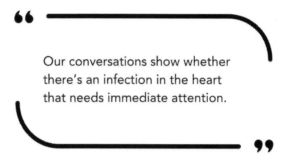

> Our conversations show whether there's an infection in the heart that needs immediate attention.

Awareness of this truth, combined with the Holy Spirit's conviction over something inappropriate I had said, inspired the "Words from the Heart" poem.

Guidelines for Daily Conversation

Ephesians 4:29 teems with practical guidelines that help me evaluate my daily conversations. More than once, the Holy Spirit has reminded me of this verse and prevented me from sinning with what I was about to say. He has also used this verse to prompt me to speak words of encouragement or comfort to someone: "Let no unwholesome word proceed from your mouth, but only such a word as is good for edification, according to the need of the moment, that it may give grace to those who hear" (NASB).

"Unwholesome" speech refers to impure or coarse language, as well as to any word that's inappropriate or unfit for the occasion. Words that promote "edification" build up, inspire or encourage someone. "According to the need of the moment" refers to timely words that help meet a need in either the person hearing us, or in a third party about whom we're talking.

The term "gracious" suggests that God expects us to treat others better than they deserve with our words—a helpful guideline when we are talking to or about someone who has hurt or mistreated us. By delving into the background of key words in Ephesians 4:29, I formulated these questions to assist me in evaluating my conversations.

- Are my words impure or unwholesome, unfit for this occasion?
- Do my words build up or tear down the person to whom or about whom I'm talking?
- Do these words meet a need in the person to whom or about whom I'm talking?
- Do my words give grace to the person with whom or about whom I'm speaking?

? Probes to Ponder

What do recent conversations at work, among friends, at home and over the phone reveal about the state of your heart? Have you said anything that requires confession before God or to another person?

Glance again at the four questions based on Ephesians 4:29. Which of the four guidelines for conversation is the Holy Spirit nudging you to apply today?

On a positive note, as you read the four conversational guidelines, dd the Holy Spirit bring someone to mind who needs a word of comfort or encouragement from you?

 Prayer Response

Father, I can't think of what to say to You about sins of my tongue that's any more appropriate than what King David prayed in Psalm 19:14. So as I repeat his utterance to You today, please work within me to make it happen: "Let the words of my mouth and the meditation of my heart be acceptable in your sight O Lord, my rock and my redeemer." In the name of Your Son, the only person who never sinned with words, amen.

 A Pertinent Word

Let your speech always be gracious, seasoned with salt, so that you may know how you ought to answer each person.

Colossians 4:6

 An Apt Quote

If your lips would keep from slips

five things observe with care:

to whom you speak, of whom you speak,

and how, and when, and where.[1]

—William Norris

TEN

DO YOU LISTEN WITH YOUR HEART?

Listening with Your Heart

While I am conversing
most folks are rehearsing
what they plan to convey.
They don't hear what I say.

They squirm quite a bit
as they stand or sit.
Or flash wordless information
that their thoughts are on vacation.
Or their eyes indicate
that they are running late.

Yet when I'm talking to you,
I get a different view.
I can see from your expression
that my words are your obsession.
Yes, you practice the fine art

of listening with your heart.
Oh, wouldn't it be grand
if everybody would
seek first to understand;
then to be understood.

———

More than a Comma

During a chat with his youth pastor, a teenager described how he felt when he tried to talk to his dad.

"You know what I am?" said the teen. "I'm a comma. I'll be talking to my dad and he'll say something. Then when I start to talk, he pauses. He doesn't interrupt, but when I'm through he starts up again right where he left off. What I say doesn't really mean anything. I'm just a comma in his monolog."

How sobering it is to realize that even if we never interrupt someone, we still may not listen well. The father heard with his ears as his son talked, but he didn't listen with his heart. He didn't react to anything his son said.

Listening is more than a noble social skill. It's a way of assigning worth to another person, of showing dignity.

I wrote "Listening with Your Heart" for a friend who listens well. I never feel like a comma in her presence.

Hearing More Than Words

When we listen with our hearts, we're conscious of what a person conveys through all three modes of communication: *actual words, tone of voice* and *nonverbal signals.* Experts on communication theory insist that how a person says something packs much more wallop than what he or she says. As noted in the following image, 7% of a person's actual message is conveyed through words, 38% through tone of voice and 55% through the body's nonverbal signals.[1]

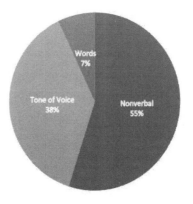

Imagine: a person's words account for a small percentage of what he or she is actually saying to us! To listen well to all three modes of communication necessarily involves listening with our hearts. And heart listening requires eye contact, focused attention, nods that we're tracking with the person's story, and a limited number of carefully selected words that prompt the other person to say more, if needed.

Similarly, how the other person perceives *our* message during a conversation depends on what *we* communicate through all three modes: actual words, tone of voice and nonverbal signals. What are we conveying nonverbally through eye contact and other forms of focused attention? How does the other person perceive our tone of voice?

Probes to Ponder

When you read about the three modes of communication, what reactions did you have? Why?

To become a person who "listens with the heart," what specific changes do you need to make?

Identify one personal relationship in which you yearn for more intimacy or better communication. If you grow in your capacity to listen well to this person, how will it show?

Prayer Response

Father, when Your Son met people as He moved about in Palestine, He listened well, even to those who interrupted Him. Create in me more Christlikeness in this regard. Give me a capacity for focused attention as people talk, to listen with my eye contact as well as with my ears. Enable me to hear not only each word they say to me, but to grasp what they're communicating nonverbally as well. In the name of the Savior, who heard what a person's heart said, amen.

A Pertinent Word

If one gives an answer before he hears, it is his folly and shame.

Proverbs 18:13

 An Apt Quote

In her book *Real Friends*, Barbara Varenhorst explained how caring for others is a prerequisite to heart listening:

> Heart listening can be learned, but it cannot be practiced or done mechanically. You can listen mechanically with your ears, but not with your heart. Why? Because the essence of listening with your heart is to put your whole self into trying to hear what the other person is saying, because you care that much. Unless you care, you won't stop talking, resisting, or ignoring long enough to hear what is being said. You won't sacrifice your time or convenience to hear the other person's feelings behind the words or twisted behaviors. If you care enough, you will learn the necessary skills, and then you will practice repeatedly, putting out the effort needed to learn to "listen with your heart."[2]

ELEVEN
ARE YOU WAVING A WHITE FLAG?

White Flag

My uniform: blood-stained and torn.
My spirit, too, is battle-worn.
My body aches. My frail hopes sag.
That's why I'm waving a white flag.

This war I've waged for years on end.
I've no more energy to spend.
I've suffered only loss and pain
by trying to resist Your reign.

Corpses dot this killing field.
No more weapons do I wield.
Besides, I'm out of ammunition.
How I loathe this grave condition!

You offered terms, but I refused.
The result? I'm scarred and bruised.

I'm giving up the stubborn quest
for medals pinned upon my chest.

All of my defenses crumbled.
Now I'm broken-hearted, humbled
by the fact I can't succeed
unless You, Jesus, take the lead.

So take this offer of my sword.
I yield to You, O Sovereign Lord.
Choose for me an unmarked grave;
or, if preferred, I'll be Your slave.

Lock me in a ball and chain
if You think I'll rebel again.
Or throw me in a dungeon deep,
where on cold stone I'll try to sleep.

O Master, did I hear You right?
Your yoke easy? Your burden light?
Instead of punishment my lot,
You hold my past against me not?
Instead of prisoner, You dare
to call me "son," say I'm an heir?
That since my heart is now tender,
*I'll view this as a **glad surrender**?*

———

Raising a White Flag

One expression of surrender in previous generations characterized by trench warfare was "waving a white flag." To hoist a white flag from a bunker, within view of the opposing forces, was a way of saying, "Don't shoot! We give up! We surrender!"

I employed a battlefield analogy in the poem. The issue in this poem is *not* the surrender of initially giving my life to Christ, of putting my faith in Him as Savior. These lyrics refer to the daily need for His followers to surrender to His Lordship and will. My main idea is to show that any such submission to Him is ultimately for *our* good, and we'll view it as a *glad surrender.*

Understanding Surrender

Long ago, when the primary battlefield weapon was a sword instead of high-powered rifles or computer-controlled missiles, a commander whose troops won a battle met with the leader of the defeated army, who agreed to surrender. The vanquished foe walked up to the victor and offered him his hand. The winner refused to shake hands.

"First your sword, then your hand!" said the conqueror.

The loser dropped his sword at the feet of the victor.[1]

What a riveting example of the meaning of surrender!

To drop all weapons or means of resistance.

To resign oneself to defeat.

To give up in favor of another.

To abandon all hope of coming out on top.

To bring nothing to the table when it comes to negotiations.

To relinquish one's personal goals, ambitions and possessions to the authority of another.

I understand surrender when I realize that I can't say "No, Lord!" and mean both words!

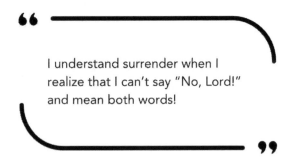

66

I understand surrender when I
realize that I can't say "No, Lord!"
and mean both words!

99

How Does Surrender Show?

I recall that battlefield story when I consider my life in relation to Jesus' lordship. What does (or should) unconditional surrender look like for me? Here are a few possible answers.

- *To rein in my long-held desire to write a "best-selling" Christian book.* To confess the envy I feel when someone else does it, especially when I know him or her personally. To thank the Lord for the significant platform He has already given me, and leave the expansion of the borders of my influence in His hands.

- *To stop complaining day in and day out about my chronic back pain.* Sure it hurts, but I don't have to let everyone know. I often comment to my wife about how bad it is, which doesn't enhance the atmosphere around the house. A colleague whose physical pain dwarfs mine once told me, "I can't control whether I hurt, but I can control my attitude."

- *To heed the Lord's strong "inside whisper" when He wants me to give financially to someone in need.* To stop rationalizing a refusal by citing my tight budget.

- *To submit to God's sovereignty when it comes to depression and how He has put me together emotionally.* This form of surrender doesn't mean I don't strive for better mental health. If the mood plummets to such an extent that I can't function well, I may once again try the common graces of medical intervention and counseling. What it does mean, though, is that I stop bucking the hypersensitive spirit I've had since birth, that I keep asking God to sustain me and for Him to redeem the pain so I better serve others.

What inspires me to surrender daily to God's will is recollection of Jesus' own submission to the Father's plan for Him to die on the cross in our place. Jesus prayed for the cup of suffering to be removed, but He concluded, "Yet not what I will, but what you will" (Mark 14:36).

Christ's surrender to the cross assures us that our moments of surrender will also result in a redemptive outcome.

Probes to Ponder

If you were to approach your Master and surrender, unconditionally, what would it look like? What areas of your life would change as a result?

In the poem lyrics I cite painful consequences of controlling my life. What negative consequences have you experienced by failing to surrender completely to the Lord?

Identify times you've yielded control of something or someone to the Lord. What did you gain by raising a white flag in those instances? How did that experience become a *glad surrender*? If you hesitate to surrender an area of your life to the Lord, what does that hesitancy say about your view of God and His character?

Prayer Response

Oh Father, help me to realize that what I give up by surrendering to You each day can't match what I gain. In the name of Your Son, who yielded to death on a cross only to be exalted, amen.

A Pertinent Word

Why do you call me "Lord, Lord," and not do what I tell you?

Luke 6:46

An Apt Quote

True prayer, by definition, is an act of surrender—the antidote to grasping for control (and the anxiety produced by such striving). We don't need to live in denial or disillusionment; we only need to understand prayer as an act of surrender to our tender Abba, not as a means to control our world.[2]

—Scotty Smith, *Searching for Grace*

TWELVE

WILL YOU ASK GOD TO SEARCH YOUR HEART?

Search My Heart

Please search my heart with Spirit's light.
Throughout it look for the blight
of hidden sin in any form.
Probe deep within until the norm
is a new reign that sets me free
from ways of pain that hinder me.

What You expose will threaten hell.
My spirit knows Satan will rail
against this threat to long-held throne.
But I don't fret. I'm not alone;
for You will wage the war within
that quells his rage, and You will win!

My heart without Your Spirit's gaze
is plagued by doubt and selfish ways;
by petty greed and foolish lust;

by strong felt need that always must
be catered to. It's so absurd.
I can't see You or hear Your Word.
So Spirit, reveal all hurtful ways
until Your purifying rays
revive me, and it is not strange
that my heart be a place of change.
Take what's impure and caused me shame.
Be my allure. Exalt Your name.

———

Painful Exposure

What generated the poem was time I spent meditating on and memorizing Psalm 139:23-24, one of King David's prayers. "Search me O God, and know my heart! Try me and know my thoughts! And see if there be any grievous way in me, and lead me in the way everlasting." The literal meaning of "grievous way" is "way of pain."

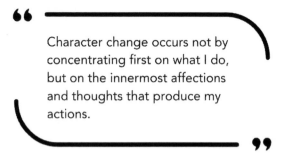

Character change occurs not by concentrating first on what I do, but on the innermost affections and thoughts that produce my actions.

I began praying those words, too. Like David, I recognized that spiritual renewal occurs from the inside-out. Character change occurs not by concentrating first on what I do, but on the innermost affections and thoughts that produce my actions. As Proverbs 21:2 points out, "Every way of a man is right in his own eyes, but the Lord weighs the heart."

In the bold prayer of those verses, I pleaded with the Lord to expose anything embedded in my heart that grieved Him, contaminated my relationships or tarnished my character. God's answer to that prayer involved painful exposure to selfish attitudes and misplaced affections residing in my heart. During the weeks I prayed these verses regularly, I became increasingly conscious of a tendency to stretch the truth; of impure thoughts that I had rationalized as being "par for the course" for men, and of self-centered attitudes that hindered intimacy with people close to me. It was as if all hell broke loose in my heart!

What was God up to?

In reference to the words in Psalm 139:23-24, He had to expose hurtful ways in me before He could "lead me in the way everlasting." He beamed His Spirit's light on sins that I had been tolerating far too long. He answered my prayer by making me more sensitive to the impurities, and I didn't like what I saw! Yet their exposure led to heartfelt, tears-inducing bouts of confession, an inner state that nudged me closer to that elusive goal called purity.

I just didn't know that things would get worse before they'd get better, that His uprooting of painful ways would, ironically, hurt so much. But it was similar to the pain of surgery to remove a cancerous tumor. The temporary discomfort of surgical wounds often results in a healthier, more vibrant body.

? Probes to Ponder

Why is there a tendency in us to ask God to change our circumstances or behavior, rather than to transform our affections and attitudes?

Have you experienced a time of spiritual renewal or cleansing that began with turmoil or pain? Did you thank the Lord for the Holy Spirit's painful conviction?

Why does spiritual warfare—some form of Satanic opposition —occur whenever you plea for God to search your heart?

What are the risks of *not* asking the Lord to search your heart?

Prayer Response

Oh Father, when I'm first prompted to ask You to search my heart, I feel a niggling discomfort—even a measure of resistance —deep down in my spirit. Why? Is it because I secretly enjoy certain sins too much and don't really want to give them up? Do I fear the offensive that Satan will initiate in an effort to thwart Your transforming work? Am I too comfortable with the idols stashed in the dark corners of my heart, and I don't like the idea of losing them? I'm admitting my hesitancy to You, yet please—for my ultimate good and Your glory in and through me—heed my plea to search and to cleanse my heart. I'll be glad—very glad!— with the outcomes: greater intimacy with You and escalating fruitfulness for Your Kingdom. In the name of Your Son, the only person who ever lived who didn't need to pray, "Search my heart," amen.

A Pertinent Word

Create in me a clean heart, O God, and renew a right spirit within me.

Psalm 51:10

66 99 An Apt Quote

Grace explodes on us with penetrating, heart-exposing light. Grace illumines our dark hallways and our dark corners. The Son of grace shines the light of his grace into the darkest recesses of our hearts, not as an act of vengeance or punishment, but as a move of forgiving, transforming, and delivering grace. He dispels our self-inflicted darkness because he knows that we cannot grieve what we do not see, we cannot confess what we have not grieved, and we cannot turn from what we haven't confessed.[1]

—Paul Tripp

THIRTEEN
WILL YOU PRAY, "LORD, SEND A REVIVAL"?

Revive My Heart

I don't always play it smart
with the affections of my heart.
The world's values eclipse the Son.
Instead of Him second to none,
I believe lies and clutch but toys,
leaving unclaimed much greater joys
that only life with God bestows.
Then my dissatisfaction grows.

Keep me from seeking my own fame.
Use me to glorify Your name.
Revive my heart until it's pure.
Yes, wean me from the world's allure,
from vain pursuits, deceitful lust.
Discipline me, Lord, if you must.
Purge impure thoughts; renew my mind,
so I will not be as inclined

to view sin as tempting delight
that I yield to without a fight.
Revive my heart. I don't care how.
Break it, Father, until I bow
my knees before Your throne of grace
and tears for sin drop down my face.

I'll be a man who's much deprived
until my selfish heart's revived.
The pleasure words cannot explain
comes only when, under Your reign,
I'm intimate with You, Oh God.
So it is good if painful rod
motivates me to do my part.
Spark renovation of my heart.

―――――

This plea for personal revival echoes the theme of the previous chapter. Asking God to "revive my heart" is similar to asking Him to "search my heart." Both chapters emphasize that personal renewal is an inside-out phenomenon. Heart change necessarily precedes behavioral transformation.

> Heart change necessarily precedes behavioral transformation. A prerequisite for revival is the Holy Spirit's "heart work" within me.

A prerequisite for revival is the Holy Spirit's "heart work" within me. As the lyrics show, I asked Him to pull out by the roots all sin patterns that impeded my spiritual formation and usefulness to Him.

When God sparks renovation in the heart of His people, the likelihood of a broader corporate revival in the church increases.

Holy Ground

"I'm standing on holy ground!"

That's what I thought and felt as awe concerning a work of God enveloped me. I stood on an earthen floor between crumbling walls of what had been a one-room church building in the rural Risitu region of Zimbabwe, Africa (formerly Southern Rhodesia).

A much larger sanctuary stood within view, but I wanted to visit the shell of the older one for a prayer time.

Why?

Earlier that day, I read several pages in a book that described a revival in Africa that began in 1915 on the very spot where I stood. During the first week of a visiting evangelist's messages, not much happened. But he taught the people a chorus which they sang in every meeting. The lyrics included this refrain: *"Lord, send a revival, and let it start with me."*

As the days progressed, people who learned the chorus sang it throughout the day. As they walked from place to place, toiled in the fields or cooked in their tiny homes, they kept repeating in song, "Lord, send a revival, and let it start with me."

Their prayers in the form of song lyrics warmed the heart of God. As the book author put it, one night during a service, "the Holy Spirit fell." Weeping erupted. Heartfelt conviction crushed the hearts of believers, spawning public confession of sin as well as apologies to people they had wronged within the congregation. Unbelievers responded to the Spirit's wooing by putting their faith in Christ.

A few people, compelled by the Spirit's insistence to get right with God, ran to the altar and dropped to their knees. One person who stormed to the front accidentally banged into the evangelist. Meetings continued for fifteen months. The evangelist God used to spark the revival later preached at 25 other African mission stations. During a five-year period, over 10,000 individuals surrendered to Jesus Christ for salvation.[1]

As I recalled the story, my heart ached over the lethargy of spirit that characterized many churches back in the United States. Then the Holy Spirit shifted my attention away from churches to the need within my own heart. He whispered, "Terry, *you* need to sing that chorus—and mean it! Revival starts in the heart of My people."

As I stood within that ruined sanctuary shell, I spotted on the ground a baseball-sized, roseate stone that had been part of the inside wall. I took it back home, placing it on my office shelf to remind me to insert these lyrics into my prayer times: "Lord, send a revival, and let it start with me."

Enduring Characteristics of Revival

David Mains, a student of revival movements throughout church history, cited three enduring characteristics of authentic revival: concentrated, corporate prayer for spiritual awakening; tears and brokenness over sin on the part of God's people, and widespread conversions precipitated by repentance among believers.[2] All three phenomena occurred in Risitu.

Like the Risitu Christians of a previous generation, my primary reason to lament must always be *my* need for holiness, not the bleak moral climate of my community or nation.

As I write this, I glance at the rock on my shelf. I whisper, "Oh God, break my heart over sin. Forgive me for taking my sin too casually, for hurting You and thinking so little of Jesus' death for it. Please, God, don't let me sin successfully. Either embarrass me by letting me get caught or convict me until my heart bleeds and tears pour down my face."

? Probes to Ponder

How can you tell when genuine spiritual revival occurs in an individual? In a local church? In a nation?

Look again at the enduring characteristics of revival cited by David Mains. How should these manifestations of revival affect how you pray for it? Within your personal life and your church, what factors stymie the progression of these phenomena?

As you yearn for revival in your local church, community and nation, will you start with a plea for revival in your own heart?

Prayer Response

Father, my prayer today starts with lyrics to a song containing the same heartfelt plea of the chorus sung back in 1915 by the residents of Risitu:

> *It's me, it's me, O Lord,*
> *standing in the need of prayer.*
> *It's me, it's me, O Lord,*
> *standing in the need of prayer.*
> *Not my brother, not my sister,*
> *but it's me, O Lord,*
> *standing in the need of prayer.*
> *Not the preacher, not the deacon,*
> *but it's me, O Lord,*
> *standing in the need of prayer.*
> *Not my father, not my mother,*
> *but it is me, O Lord,*
> *standing in the need of prayer.[3]*

*Oh, may I sing those lyrics and really mean them! Graciously do what You need to do **to** me, so You can do what You want to do **through** me. In the name of the only Person who ever walked the earth who didn't need a revival in His heart, amen.*

A Pertinent Word

If my people who are called by my name humble themselves, and pray and seek my face and turn from their wicked ways, then I will hear from heaven and will forgive their sin and heal their land.

2 Chronicles 7:14

❝❞ An Apt Quote

You and I will never know God in revival until we first meet Him in brokenness.[4]

—Nancy Demoss Wolgemuth, *Brokenness, Surrender, Holiness*

FOURTEEN
IS "CONVICTING GRACE" AN OXYMORON?

Break My Heart

*I did not place relentless guard
over my heart, so it grew hard.
Oh, Father, please do not forsake it.
Send your Spirit force to break it.*

*Crush the things that don't belong:
the pride that's blind to all the wrong;
the impure thoughts to which I'm prone;
the yearning for things I don't own.*

*Root out the reign of my felt need
and in its place plant fruitful seed
that grows best when ground is broken.
Then I'll know that You have spoken.*

*Only when my hopes have crumbled,
when I'm broken-hearted, humbled,*

will I yield to Your Spirit's reign.
A pure heart only comes through pain.

So break my heart until the sin
that now feels much at home within
leaves speedily through all the cracks
made when Your heavy hand attacks.

———

A Painful Gift

This is the third consecutive chapter in which I deal with the heart. The first contained my plea for God to *search my heart* and remove ways of pain. The second asked God to *revive my heart*, since revival in the church starts with personal pleas for renewal. This chapter invites God to *break my heart* so I'm not satisfied with the status quo in my life.

The "Break My Heart" poem is a way of asking for the Holy Spirit's conviction, which is a prerequisite for repentance. All three poems focus on the need for inside-out change, but this chapter zeroes in on the inevitable pain involved when the Holy Spirit convicts us of sin.

Novelist George MacDonald wrote, "The only thing that improves by breaking it is the human heart."[1] The Holy Spirit's conviction instills a loathing of sin. We grieve not only due to the hurtful consequences of our sin, but because we've hurt the one who sacrificed His life for ours. When we start taking our sin too casually, it's time to plead with God to break our hearts over it.

When we sin against God or others, His conviction should pierce us and cause pain that compels us to confess. This temporary pain shows us our sin with greater clarity and drives us to depend more than ever on the Lord's strength for daily living. His conviction restrains our sinful impulses, preventing worse pain and more dreadful consequences if we remained tethered to the sinful pattern. Put simply, *His conviction is a grace!*

Charles Spurgeon, citing the necessity of sorrow over sin as well as the exuberance we should feel over forgiveness, wrote, "Since Christ died for me, I cannot trifle with the sin which killed my best Friend. There are two kinds of tears that Christians shed: one is the tear of sorrow because of sin; the other is a tear of joy because of pardon."[2]

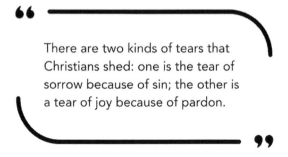

There are two kinds of tears that Christians shed: one is the tear of sorrow because of sin; the other is a tear of joy because of pardon.

Story of Convicting Grace

Joe Bayly wrote a captivating article titled, "Why Don't Sinners Cry Anymore?" He lamented the absence of brokenness and tears that should accompany conviction of sin.

British thinker and preacher Martyn Lloyd-Jones once commented that people no longer weep at evangelistic meetings. They laugh, he said, they happily come to the front but they don't mourn over their sins....

Godly sorrow for sin that leads to repentance is almost totally absent from our preaching and our lives. The one who enters the kingdom without repentance hardly finds need for it as a resident. We have lost the ability to say "I'm sorry" to God and to one another. We have lost it as persons and we have lost it in our churches and we have lost it as a nation....

Joseph C. Macaulay told of a visit to the Hebrides Islands some years ago, when revival was going on. On his way to the church, where he was to preach, Dr. Macaulay heard a man sobbing in a cottage as he passed.

"What's that?" he asked his companion.

"That's John. He's on his way to God. He'll come through," was the reply.[3]

The island native was under conviction that propelled him to put his faith in Christ for salvation. But a similar experience may also be needed when the Holy Spirit convicts a Christian for a pattern of sin that he has been treating too casually. In a warning against worldliness creeping into the lives of recent converts to Christ, James emphasized the need for repentance accompanied by mourning and weeping: "Cleanse your hands, you sinners, and purify your hearts, you double-minded. Be wretched and mourn and weep. Let your laughter be turned into mourning and your joy to gloom" (James 4:8-9).

When was the last time you heard a sermon to church members on those verses?

? Probes to Ponder

When Christ-followers take their sin too casually, how does their indifference show? Why is flippancy toward our sin treacherous? Are you taking a particular area of disobedience too casually? Dare you pray, "Lord, break my heart"? How is the Holy Spirit's conviction a *grace*? If someone asked you that question, how would you respond?

Prayer Response

Father, please don't let me sin successfully. Break my heart with Your Spirit's conviction so I never want to hurt that much ever again. In the name of Jesus, whose heart broke over others' sin, but never over His own, amen.

A Pertinent Word

When you're under conviction of sin, this promise offers encouragement: "If we say we have no sin, we deceive ourselves, and the truth is not in us. If we confess our sins, he is faithful and just to forgive us our sins and to cleanse us from all unrighteousness."

1 John 1:8-9

❝❞   An Apt Quote

Elyse Fitzpatrick explains why the Holy Spirit's conviction should never result in self-condemnation:

> There is a significant difference between conviction brought about by the Spirit and self-condemnation brought about by the Accuser (Satan). Conviction of sin draws me away from myself and toward God; it frees me to repent, grants me sorrow over offending my King, and floods me with relief in knowing that his smile still rests upon me. It eventuates in my loving Jesus more. Self-condemnation, on the other hand, draws me down into myself and away from God. It makes me afraid and distrustful of him. It entraps me in unrelenting self-loathing and unbelief. Self-condemnation doesn't make me love Jesus more, because it is not necessarily about him. It's about me.[4]

—Elyse Fitzpatrick

FIFTEEN
HOW CAN YOU BEST GLORIFY GOD?

How?

How can God receive most glory
in the plot of my life's story?
When I teach a class with flair
or stop to show someone I care?
When I apply truth that I've heard
or work to memorize His Word?
When I explain why I believe
to people willing to receive?
When I give away my stuff
to those who don't have enough?
When I gladly pay the price
for some need-meeting sacrifice?
When others read the words I write
and benefit from my insight?
When my faith gets off the fence?
I start my day with confidence?

Or is the Lord more magnified
when my feeble hands are tied?
When I am mired knee-deep in need
and I've no recourse but to plead
for Him to rewrite my life's plot,
and do for me what I cannot?
When I'm trapped at my wit's end
and I've no choice but to depend
on wisdom I do not possess
to respond wisely to distress?
Or when the devil turns up heat
and I am one step from defeat,
yearning for him to desist;
pleading for strength to resist?

Or when despondency descends;
I stumble in the fog it sends,
and the light can't penetrate,
and I groan under the weight
of a spirit without hope;
when I need Christ just to cope?
Or when I'm flat upon my face
relying on sustaining grace,
weaned from pointless human pride?
Is that when He's most glorified?
When only what the Lord can do
erases fear and sees me through?

Yes, His power gives me a song,
for when I'm weak, then He is strong!
Yes, His name is lifted up
when I extend my empty cup.

Reassurance for Needy People

There's a tendency to think that we glorify God best through some avenue of service or a demonstration of uncompromising character. No doubt we honor Him in those ways, but an irony of Christian living is that *God gets most glory when we're needy, when we're in a situation that needs a divine remedy.*

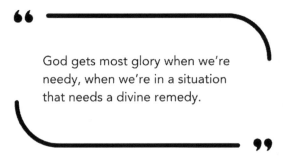

> God gets most glory when we're needy, when we're in a situation that needs a divine remedy.

Sad to say, it's often only when we feel weak and needy that we cry out to God. Due to the limits of our resourcefulness, we're prompted to pray. Then God answers our plea or displays His power in some manner. The result is...we praise Him! We tell others what God did. Put simply, God's name is most magnified when we're at wit's end and plead for God to do what only He can do. That's what the great British preacher Charles Spurgeon had in mind when he said, "We give God most glory when we get from Him most grace."[1]

More than any other truth in the Bible, this concept motivates me to pray, to seek God's help so He'll display His might and receive applause. After all, God Himself promises to help us, with the ultimate aim of receiving honor: "Call upon me in the day of trouble; I will deliver you, and you shall glorify me" (Psalm 50:15).

I'm indebted to John Piper, whose comments on Psalm 50:15 acquainted me with this truth on how God gets glory through taking our needs and weaknesses to Him. Piper insists that we glorify God "not by serving Him, but by being served by Him....We do not glorify God by providing His needs, but by praying that He would provide ours, and trusting Him to answer." According to Piper, "The Giver gets the glory. We get help."[2]

? Probes to Ponder

How do the poem and related commentary on Psalm 50:15 affect how you think about your weaknesses and needs?

How should the truth I explained affect your relationship with God?

Right now, identify a way in which you desperately need God to intervene. Will you pour out your heart to Him and ask Him to glorify Himself by doing for you what only He can do?

🐾 Prayer Response

Father, when I'm feeling helpless or needy, prompt me to call on You, to plead with You to intervene in a way that will cause You to look good. Show Your incalculable worth by doing in me or for me what only You can do. In the name of Jesus, whose primary preoccupation was to glorify You and whose death on the cross gives me access to You, amen.

 A Pertinent Word

But he said to me, "My grace is sufficient for you, for my power is made perfect in weakness." Therefore I will boast all the more gladly of my weaknesses, so that the power of Christ may rest upon me. For the sake of Christ, then, I am content with weaknesses, insults, hardships, persecutions, and calamities. For when I am weak, then I am strong.

2 Corinthians 12:9-10

 An Apt Quote

Here is a covenant that God enters into with you who pray to Him, and whom He helps. He says, "You shall have deliverance, but I must have the glory." Here is a delightful partnership; we obtain that which we so greatly need, and all that God gets is the glory which is due His name.[3]

—Charles Spurgeon's commentary on Psalm 50:15

SIXTEEN

DOES GOD HIDE A SMILE BEHIND HIS DARK PROVIDENCE?

The Hidden Smile of God

You're burdened for a precious son.
You seek answers. There are none
that satisfy, or explain why
this deed occurred. It's so absurd!

A son you raised to know the Lord,
on whom grace has been outpoured.
What happened shocks; the devil mocks.
Emotions reel and sap your zeal.

Your family has seen the scowl
of Satan's hosts upon the prowl.
The water's deep; the price is steep
that's being paid for choices made.

You feel broken-hearted, humbled.
Have your dreams for him all crumbled?

Will he hear the Master's voice
through consequences of his choice?

What will unfold I do not know,
but God is stronger than our foe.
What Satan tries is in disguise
our Lord's right hand. He's in command.

When plagued by anxious thoughts or fear,
though you don't feel Him, God is near.
His words declare that He is there;
that He'll sustain through all the pain.

You face circumstances grim.
Yet God will do what's best for him.
There is just One who loves your son
to such extent His blood was spent.

Let the tears flow. Fall on your face,
and feed upon His endless grace.
For what is now a painful rod
may mask the tender smile of God.

———

A Biblical Perspective to Prompt Prayer

Bad news jolted a couple I knew. Their son, in a drug-induced stupor, assaulted a man, resulting in a jail stint. Their son had earned a full academic scholarship to a large university, a benefit the school revoked after hearing of his arrest. The couple had raised him in a Christian home. He had graduated with honors from an academically elite Christian high school, but moving away to college affected him negatively. He succumbed to temptations and influences that in a sheltered environment had not badgered him so relentlessly.

After I heard the news, I wrote the poem to encourage them, to emphasize that God often redeems painful situations. The adverse consequences of sin often soften a person's heart and turn him or her back to God. A person's pain may wean him from self-reliance and prompt him to seek the Lord, to rely on the Lord's strength from then on.

God's Word suggests that difficulty often steers a person back to Him. The writer of Psalm 119:67 admitted, "Before I was afflicted, I went astray, but now I keep your word." Four verses later, he reiterated his point: "It is good for me that I was afflicted, that I may learn your statutes" (Psalm 119:71).

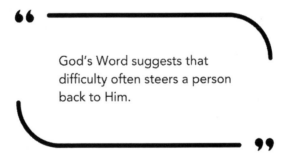

God's Word suggests that difficulty often steers a person back to Him.

I didn't know what the future held for their son, but I wanted them to keep interceding for him, because God's smile often lurks behind dark clouds of circumstance.

Neither God's Word nor this poem promises that every painful setback has a positive resolution. There's a mysterious interplay between God's part and our part, seen in how we respond to affliction. The poem and verses I quoted reveal that God is more than capable of using adversity for His glory and for our good.

For Burdened Parents

Perhaps the principle I explained in the verses from Psalm 119 and the poem lyrics will engender hope within you that God will work redemptively in the life of someone for whom you are burdened. Keep appealing fervently to the Lord. Ask God to penetrate the dark clouds accumulating over your loved one's life with a smile that symbolizes an outcome that will honor Him.

I'm a parent of two grown sons. Psalm 90:15-16 compels me to appeal to God's glory as a motivation to intercede for them. "Make us glad for as many days as you have afflicted us, and for as many years as we have seen evil. *Let your work be shown to your servants, and your glorious power to their children*" (emphasis mine).

? Probes to Ponder

Do you grieve over the plight of a grown son or daughter? Over a parent or sibling who isn't a Christ-follower, or whose choices have had devastating consequences?

Look back over your life. Do you see a time when God redeemed a poor choice you made, or employed a setback to soften your heart? If so, how does that memory motivate you to pray for someone for whom you are burdened?

Will you persist in interceding before God for this loved one? (Meditate on Luke 11:5-13, where Jesus encourages us to persist in our prayer requests.)

Prayer Response

Father, when I pray for my grown children—whether they need discernment for a decision, encouragement so they don't lose heart or spiritual renewal so they'll return to faith in You—answer it because Your intervention will result in praise and honor to You. In the name of Your Son, whose life perfectly glorified You, amen.

A Pertinent Word

Until now you have asked nothing in my name. Ask, and you will receive, that your joy may be full.

John 16:24

An Apt Quote

Through my own troubles, God has not given me explanations. But He has met me as a person, as an individual, and that's what we most need.[1]

—Elisabeth Elliot, *Suffering Is Never for Nothing*

SEVENTEEN
DO YOU WANT A MORE FRUITFUL MINISTRY?

Hero of the Faith (A Christmas Gift)

Your prayers serve as presents that money can't obtain.
We open them daily. You give them for our gain.
Not gifts displayed for everyone to see.
Not the kind found beneath a Christmas tree.
Not on the shelves of Walmart or Sears.
Instead, gifts wrapped in brokenness and tears.

Once you served up front; now, you're on your knees.
You face much more warfare, but God hears your pleas.
You plead for families when you bow your head,
that kids resist Satan and follow Christ, instead.
You set a lofty example for us to emulate.
To teach God's Word is noble, but prayer carries more weight.

Prayer is your stay; the Bible is your sword.
You intercede for the church, the bride of the Lord.
Keep interceding while God still has you around.

The floor or bed where you pray, God views as holy ground.
You have finished well. These words are long overdue:
you're a hero of the faith, and I thank the Lord for you.

———

Intercessor Extraordinaire

I wrote this poem in the mid-1980s for a retired gentleman who had once served publicly in pastoral and missionary roles, but who, in his later years, shifted to a persistent ministry of intercession. Occasionally, our pastor at the time asked Ken Kepler to come forward and lead in prayer for special needs in the congregation. When he prayed, I always felt an overwhelming sense of the Holy Spirit's presence. With my mind's eye, I could see Satan and his minions fleeing the sanctuary during Ken's prayers.

I visited his home to give him photos of my two young sons, for whom he pledged to pray. After his wife died, loneliness enveloped him. His own body became frail. He was in and out of the hospital for several years. More than once I heard him say that he wanted to go home (to heaven). He didn't understand why God wouldn't heed his request.

Though his physical health waned, his mind remained clear. On Christmas day, a couple of years before he died, I visited Ken in the hospital. I gave him the poem and explained that God kept him around because of the vital intercessory prayers he offered daily.

Fruitful Intercession

Typically, we associate "ministry" with vocational Christian workers or with serious volunteers who teach church classes, or who regularly share their faith with unbelievers.

Yet intercessory prayer may be the most significant form of ministry available to Christ-followers. Since no spiritual gift is a prerequisite, it's a service outlet available to every Christian. Nor does intercession require a degree in Bible. Often, intercession isn't practiced in public venues that involve an up-front role. Even though intercession is a taken-for-granted service outlet, whoever exercises this ministry is harder to replace than preachers or missionaries or Bible study leaders.

The most irreplaceable people are those who regularly pray for lost loved ones, for their pastoral staff, for missionaries their church supports, for marriages they know that are in trouble —you name it!

> **"** The most irreplaceable people are those who regularly pray for lost loved ones, for their pastoral staff, for missionaries their church supports, for marriages they know that are in trouble—you name it! **"**

Intercession in Scripture

Serious intercession requires discipline, a firm conviction that God answers prayer, love for people, and humility. Though fruitful intercession may occur when we meet with others, most of it happens in private, where we receive no accolades or compliments to fuel our egos. Let's examine four intercessors in the Bible.

Epaphras' Intercession

Paul expressed keen appreciation for a little-known Bible character, Epaphras, a member of the church in Colossae who had visited Paul: "Epaphras, who is one of you, a servant of Christ Jesus, greets you, always struggling on your behalf in his prayers, that you may stand mature and fully assured in all the will of God" (Colossians 4:12).

The original term translated *struggling* meant to wrestle, to agonize. To intercede earnestly for others is a front-line battle of spiritual warfare. Not many people line up for the position of prayer warrior.

Nehemiah's Intercession

Before Nehemiah organized a remnant of God's people to rebuild the wall around Jerusalem, he heard of their troubling circumstance and vulnerability to attack. His heart broke over their plight. He mourned, wept, and fasted for days, "praying before the God of heaven" (Nehemiah 1:4). Nehemiah's heartfelt intercession led to God's call for him to get directly involved in their desperate need. (Examine the summary of his prayer in Nehemiah 1:5-11. Look for characteristics of an intercessor as well as guidelines for the content elements of intercessory prayer.)

Jesus' Intercession

When Jesus told Peter to expect attacks from Satan, He added, "but I have prayed for you that your faith may not fail" (Luke 22:31-32). John 17 contains Jesus' high priestly prayer. He interceded for His current disciples as well as for future generations of believers. Jesus still prays for His earthly followers! Paul insisted that He's currently at the right hand of God the Father, "interceding for us" (Romans 8:34).

Paul's Intercession

In almost every letter Paul wrote, he told the person or church group that he prayed for them. To the Ephesians he said, "I do not cease to give thanks for you, remembering you in my prayers" (1:16). Also, "I bow my knees before the Father....that he may grant you to be strengthened with power through His Spirit in your inner being" (3:14-16). To the Thessalonians he wrote that he and his team were "constantly mentioning you in our prayers" (1:2). In those representative samples, Paul went on to cite specific things he brought before God on their behalf.

Paul received as well as gave intercessory prayer. After he told members of the Ephesian church to pray for each other, he asked them to pray "for me, that words may be given to me in opening my mouth boldly to proclaim the mystery of the gospel" (6:18-19).

Obviously, God's Word suggests that passion, giftedness and hard work aren't sufficient without appeals to God for the people we serve or want to influence. No vocational or volunteer ministry is solely a human endeavor.

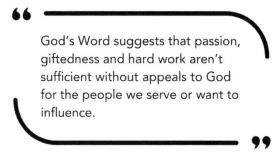

> God's Word suggests that passion, giftedness and hard work aren't sufficient without appeals to God for the people we serve or want to influence.

? Probes to Ponder

What person, family, local church or ministry organization is God's Spirit calling you to serve more frequently through intercession?

If, like Epaphras, you begin *struggling* to serve others through prayer, how will your schedule change? Where in your schedule will you find a few minutes each day for intercession?

Do you have a brother or sister in Christ, or a small group of believers, who intercede for you? Are you willing to be transparent about your personal needs or family stressors so the requests you share aren't superficial ones?

If you're in vocational Christian ministry, what are you doing to maximize the amount of intercessory prayer you receive?

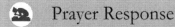 Prayer Response

Adapt the words of my prayer to your own situation:

Father, I labor earnestly, long and hard, when I prepare for a new sermon or classroom teaching session. When I write, I revise everything several times and strive to find just the right words and analogies. That's because I believe those ministries teem with potential. But I can't say that, like Epaphras, I am "always struggling" in prayer for others. My intercessory prayers are too infrequent, too perfunctory. Oh, forgive me for my unbelief and for the pride behind my tendency to focus more on public ministry venues than on private, behind-the-scenes intercession. In the name of Your Son, who didn't just teach His disciples, but who prayed fervently for them, amen.

 ## A Pertinent Word

From a public address by the prophet Samuel to the people of Israel (especially relevant to today's Christian leaders):

Moreover, as for me, far be it from me that I should sin against the Lord by ceasing to pray for you.

1 Samuel 12:23

 ## An Apt Quote

If we truly love people, we will desire for them far more than it is within us to give them, and this leads us to prayer.[1]

—Richard Foster, *Prayer: Finding the Heart's True Home*

EIGHTEEN

WHAT THREATENS THE SURVIVAL OF YOUR MARRIAGE?

Marriage Metaphor

Lush leaves, a tree's jade dress,
dance with the wind's caress.
Then with fall, a change in color:
first, leaves appear much duller.
Then gold or red bleeds from the stem,
draining leaves of all their vim.
Next, a stiff breeze overwhelms.
See them severed from their limbs.
We scrunch them beneath our toes.
Brown. Brittle. They decompose.

Verdant love pulsates with life
between a man and his wife.
Then the autumn years arrive.
Will the warmth of love survive?
When wrinkles show and they're not slim,
will the glow of vows grow dim?

Will dull routine and things mundane
erode the green and leave just stain?
Will the harsher winds sever
what God intends to last forever?
Like oak leaves, will love take flight?
Make the earth its burial site?

No! True love has its reasons
to thrive in changing seasons.
Not oak, maple or Bradford pear.
True love is what cedars wear!

Oak or Cedar?

Whether a marriage flourishes or flounders depends on whether the marriage is analogous to the foliage of an oak tree or that of a cedar. The oak's leaves turn brown and fall to the ground in the autumn, but the cedar sprouts green shoots year-round. The poem expands the tree analogy a bit further.

The poem begins by describing the life cycle of leaves on most hardwood trees. Verdant leaves turn into eye-popping, roseate colors in autumn, before turning brown and falling off their limbs. Then I compare a marriage that dies in middle age to those leaves. Finally, I compare a strong marriage to greenery that doesn't die or change colors with the onset of cooler weather, such as the green dress of a cedar.

Threats to Survival

Marriage exposes one's character before it starts developing one's character. The years constituting middle age and beyond are particularly revealing. That's when the kids are in college or living on their own. Couples' schedules no longer revolve around the children's school or sports activities. The empty nest forces the man and wife to focus on each other a bit more and evaluate the status of the marriage, since it's the primary relationship they have left. The lack of focused attention on the kids enables them to see their relationship with greater clarity, whether the picture they view is positive or discouraging.

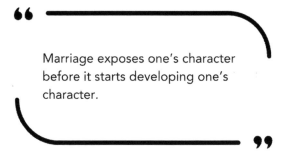

Marriage exposes one's character before it starts developing one's character.

The empty nest years bring signs of aging, causing alarm to the extent a person has relied on looks or physical prowess for a sense of significance. It's during this phase of life that a marriage either deteriorates or grows stronger, depending on the foundation laid in earlier years and the values that control the man and wife.

Hopefully, marriage between Christians will echo the qualitative relationship reflected in one husband's praise of his wife in Proverbs 31:10-11: "An excellent wife who can find? She is far more precious than jewels. The heart of her husband trusts in her, and he will have no lack of gain."

A Word of Grace

Satan directs hatred toward two entities: Jesus Christ and members of His church. Christian husbands and wives wear a huge target on their backs. The enemy persistently attacks them, striving to destroy a union that serves as a representation of Christ's relationship with His bride, the church (Ephesians 5:22-33). Satan tries to besmirch Christ's reputation by destroying the marriages of Christ-followers.

In this fallen world, where indwelling sin still resides within believers (Romans 7:14-25; 1 John 1:8, 10), marriages often fail even when both the man and the woman claim faith in Christ. Sometimes both parties are culpable in the breakup. Sometimes only one partner is blameworthy and the last thing the betrayed spouse wanted was a divorce. It's crystal clear that many marriages depict the fate of the oak's leaves, rather than the verdant dress worn by cedars.

If you're a Christ-follower who confessed failure that contributed to a divorce, rest assured that the Lord has forgiven you (1 John 1:9). Because Christ's righteousness was credited to you when you put your faith in His substitutionary death, you enjoy peace with God (Romans 5:1, 9-10). Since you are right, or justified, in His eyes, God doesn't condemn you (Romans 8:1). And fathom this: when you see Jesus' cross and its benefits clearly, you realize that God has chosen to forget any sin that contributed to the divorce. He's absent-minded (Hebrews 10:17-22)!

If you were a victim whose marriage ended through no direct fault of your own, know that the Lord appreciates the efforts you made to save the marriage. Remember that "the Lord is near to the brokenhearted and saves the crushed in spirit" (Psalm 34:18).

Also remember that a few months after leaves die and fall off their limbs, new buds form on the tree. Those buds eventually sprout new green leaves, graphically announcing the arrival of spring. Even oaks experience renewal!

In some manner, the Lord will also renew your life and relationships in a way that reflects His beauty and glory.

? Probes to Ponder

Spiritual warfare exists. Satan especially targets marriages. What are a few practical implications of this truth for your relationship with your spouse?

What can you do, individually as well as together, to defend against the inevitable attacks? (See 2 Corinthians 10:3-5.) What must happen now to increase the likelihood of finishing well together?

If you're single and desire a mate, do you regularly ask the Lord for a life partner who will love Him supremely, so he or she will love you faithfully? Do you pray often for the Lord to enrich and to sustain the marriages of people you love?

Your answer to those questions may determine whether your relationship will be analogous to the decaying leaves on an oak, or to the year-round green shoots displayed by a cedar.

Prayer Response

If you're a wife or a single person, adapt my heartfelt plea to the Lord as needed.

Father, no matter how long I've enjoyed marriage to my bride, and no matter how many decades I've known and served You, I'm still vulnerable to temptation and prone to sin. I'll never reach a spiritual plateau high enough to be invulnerable to the pull of indwelling sin. Help me to guard my heart from alien affections and the lure of other attractive women. Lord, without Your grace, grievous sin can happen to me. More than any other relationship on earth, empower me to finish well in my marriage. In the name of Your Son, whose love for the church shows me how to love my wife, amen.

A Pertinent Word

Keep your heart with all vigilance, for from it flow the springs of life.

Proverbs 4:23

An Apt Quote

A spouse might be difficult to love at times, but that's what marriage is for—to teach us how to love! Marriage cultivates our character in two ways: it teaches us to forgive and provides a context for becoming a servant.[1]

—Gary Thomas, *Sacred Marriage*

NINETEEN
HOW LONG SHOULD LOVE LAST?

As Long as Forever

How long should you love this beautiful bride?
How long should you stand by Jennifer's side?
How long is her favor too precious to lose?
How long should you hold her when she has the blues?
How long should the Lord reside in your heart,
keeping you two from growing apart?
How long should you take time for a walk?
Listen whenever she wants to talk?

How long should she smell the flowers you've sent,
and thank God for you when filled with their scent?
How long should you keep from raising your voice?
Should putting her needs first be your choice?
How long should you greet her with hugs and a kiss?
How long should she stay number one on your list?
How long should her joy be your endeavor?
The answer is simple: as long as forever.

As long as the waves lick the sand on the shore,
retreat, then repeat the cycle once more.
As long as the leaves sprout green in the spring,
turn red in autumn before they take wing.
As long as the sun arrives with the dawn,
reflecting off dew asleep on the lawn.

As long as the moon reflects the sun's light,
teams with the stars to illumine the night.
As long as sparrows serenade the trees
and puffy white clouds hitch rides with the breeze.
I'll pray for a bond that's too strong to sever.
How long should love last? As long as forever!

———

I wrote that poem for my older son, John Mark, and his fiancé. I read it aloud during the ceremony before they exchanged vows on a grassy knoll overlooking the Atlantic Ocean. He invited me to say a few words during the ceremony. For five minutes, before reading the poem, I unpacked the following statement. It may seem self-evident or even nonsensical.

Divorce is the primary reason for divorce.

What did I mean?

A Dangerous Mindset

The prevalence and acceptability of divorce in our contemporary culture makes it easier for a spouse to seek a dissolution of the marriage. Compared to previous generations, there's less stigma, less reproach associated with a marriage breakup.

Some brides and grooms approach the wedding with thoughts similar to this: "*I think he (she) will make me happy, but if it doesn't work out, I'll get a divorce. People break up all the time.*" Few individuals would admit to such a thought, but it lingers in the back of their minds, nonetheless. Perhaps that attitude explains why the divorce rate for second marriages exceeds the rate for the first one (at least 60% compared to between 40-50%). Many people with multiple divorces perpetuate the tendency to escape when things get rough.[1]

That mindset in itself increases the likelihood of eventual divorce. When inevitable conflicts occur or a person sees irritating traits or habits in a spouse that weren't as evident before they lived together, he or she is more likely to bail out of the relationship. Their mate doesn't fit their idealistic (but unrealistic) perception of the perfect spouse.

> **"** When entering a marriage, viewing divorce as a viable option keeps the husband and wife from engaging in the difficult work of ironing out differences and forgiving each other. **"**

They may repeat the traditional phrase "for better or for worse" in the ceremony, yet a firm commitment to withstand the worse is missing. When entering a marriage, viewing divorce as a viable option keeps the husband and wife from engaging in the difficult work of ironing out differences and forgiving each other. There's less resolve to keep the relationship intact.

I grin as I remember what Ruth Graham said to a reporter. Asked if she ever thought of divorce during the long marriage to Billy, her evangelist husband, she replied, *"Divorce? Never an option! Murder? Yes!"* [2]

That was Ruth's humorous, down-to-earth way of citing the iron-clad commitment she took into the marriage. She anchored her commitment to Billy in the words of Jesus: "'Therefore a man shall leave his father and his mother and hold fast to his wife, and the two shall become one flesh.' So they are no longer two but one flesh. What therefore God has joined together, let not man separate" (Matthew 19:5-6).

A Realistic Perspective

I know quite a few godly, faith-filled people who went through divorce through no fault or sin of their own. A spouse's abuse, infidelity or abandonment, along with the mate's refusal to work on healing and restoration of the relationship, resulted in termination. To save a troubled marriage requires grace-motivated effort on the part of both husband and wife.

The poem to John Mark and Jennifer was my way of encouraging them to view their marriage as a forever commitment. May our Lord enable you and your spouse, as well as your married children, to love each other for "as long as forever."

If you and your spouse demonstrate a strong commitment to the permanence of your marriage, thank God for this resolve. If not, plead with the Lord to change you and your spouse as needed. If your marriage has ended, ask your gentle Savior to keep healing your broken heart and to remove any tinge of resentment (if needed). Intercede often for the current or future marriages of your children and grandchildren.

? Probes to Ponder

I explained how the acceptability of divorce in our culture increases the likelihood of divorce. Do you agree or disagree? Why?

Whether you're currently married or hope to wed, what are some future stressors you're likely to face that could threaten the permanence of your marriage?

If you could tell an engaged couple one thing that would increase the likelihood of their marriage lasting forever, what would you say?

Prayer Response

If you're single but anticipate marriage, this prayer should still resonate with you:

O Lord, instill within my spouse and me the perseverance needed to finish well in our relationship. Let us never take for granted the indwelling sin of believers and the potential for grievous sin even in old age. And please, woo my mate and me to cultivate intimacy with You, so patterns of relational sin will not take root in our attitudes toward one another. In the name of One who said, "What God has joined together, let no man separate," amen.

 A Pertinent Word

Identify each of the descriptions or attributes of genuine love in these verses. How and when should a husband and wife demonstrate these qualities within marriage?

Love is patient and kind; love does not envy or boast; it is not arrogant or rude. It does not insist on its own way; it is not irritable or resentful; it does not rejoice at wrongdoing, but rejoices with the truth. Love bears all things, believes all things, hopes all things, endures all things.

1 Corinthians 13:4-7

 An Apt Quote

Marriage has the power to set the course of your life as a whole. If your marriage is strong, even if all the circumstances in your life around you are filled with trouble and weakness, it won't matter. You will be able to move out into the world in strength.[3]

—Tim Keller, *The Meaning of Marriage*

TWENTY
DO YOU WANT GOD TO HEAL YOUR HEART?

Heal My Hurts

When I'm absorbed too much with self
my usefulness goes on the shelf.
My attention is turned away
from folks I greet and meet each day.
Or I use them to verify
that I'm okay, a worthy guy.
Too heavily do I depend
on words of family or friend
to fill within a gaping hole,
when only God can fill that role.

Oh, God who gave me second birth,
please heal my hurts until my worth
is grounded in what Christ has done,
instead of victories I've won.
I need to change across the board.

May Your Spirit and your Sword
enable me to win at war,
so I know what You made me for:
to honor You, and You alone;
to bow before Your holy throne.

I now know that when I've relied
on folks whom I have deified
to feel secure in who I am,
I've turned my back on Christ the Lamb,
who gave His life a sacrifice,
revealing just how high a price
that He was once willing to pay
for fellowship with me someday.

Too easily my heart is broken;
too sensitive to words spoken.
Each time that people criticize,
I tend to over-analyze.
I toss and turn on sleepless nights
and readily remember slights.
My fragile ego causes pain,
yet tears I shed are all in vain
when concentration is on me,
instead of You and folks I see.
Heal my hurts; let Your Spirit start
to reconstruct this shattered heart.
Give my self-consciousness release
until I have Your perfect peace,
and I'm at home upon my face
relying on sustaining grace.

For when I bend my knees each day
I'm less prone to get in the way.
Help me focus more upon the need
of others, so I'll intercede
and heal their hurts, not thinking of
my own need for esteem or love.

For when my many hurts are healed,
then my heart will be others-filled.

Do I Love Others or Use Them?

What generated this poem was a stinging realization that I'm too self-absorbed, too prone to use others to verify my worth and significance. Though not everyone is as emotionally needy as I am, each of us is self-centered in some ways.

Do any of the following statements resonate with you?

We are often...

- More interested in others meeting our needs than in meeting the needs of others.
- More motivated by our reputation instead of God's glory.
- Relying on others' opinions of us more than God's.
- Basing our identity on our accomplishments instead of what Jesus achieved for us on the cross.

It's the fallout of our sinfulness.

Despite such tendencies, continuing erosion into greater self-centeredness isn't inevitable. A measure of healing that nudges us a bit closer to unselfishness and emotional maturity is possible if we recognize our need and plea regularly for God's enablement. The poem was my way of pleading for more emotional stability and unselfishness in my relationships. It's a plea I still pray to the Lord.

An example will clarify what I mean by relying on others to be and to do for me what only God can be and do. As I share the following story, ask God's Spirit to reveal its applicability to you. Determine the extent to which you rely excessively on others' attention to verify your worth and acceptability.

A Lesson from an Episode of Self-Pity

Something happened in my relationship with special friends that exposed my self-absorption. Brad and Kelli (not their real names) had been our best friends for years. We often ate out with them, enjoyed overnight trips together and celebrated holidays around the same table. Even after they moved out of state to launch a new, challenging ministry, we talked frequently and connected on birthdays.

One year I didn't hear from them on my birthday. No phone call or card. In a regularly scheduled visit with a counselor who treated me for depression, I told him how hurt I felt by their neglect. I vented my frustration and threw a colossal pity party! What made my reaction so juvenile was the couple's decades-long commitment to our friendship. Time and again they had demonstrated their love to my wife and to me.

The counselor helped me to see that I relied too heavily on family members and friends to meet my deep-seated need for affirmation. He explained that everyone has an emotional tank that needs filling through others' attention. He pointed out that due to my melancholy temperament and a painful abandonment by my mother during early adolescence, the capacity of my emotional tank was much larger than normal. "If the average person has a 50-gallon emotional tank capacity that needs filling," he explained, "your tank capacity is 150 gallons!" He encouraged me to be more proactive in giving to others, instead of pouting when they don't live up to my excessive expectations.

For days I pondered his admonition. I asked the Lord to help me grow emotionally, to take more initiative in meeting others' needs, starting with the couple who didn't acknowledge my recent birthday.

God's Spirit challenged me: *"Do you really love Brad and Kelli, or do you merely use them in your vain attempt to verify your own self-worth through the attention they give to you? Authentic love doesn't hinge on their response to you."*

> **"**
> Do you really love Brad and Kelli, or do you merely use them in your vain attempt to verify your own self-worth through the attention they give to you?
> **"**

A More Unselfish Love

The result was a resolve, with God's help, to send handwritten letters to Brad and Kelli twice a month. In every letter I wrote a prayer for them, wrote out a Bible verse that had sustained me in ministry, asked questions about their new ministry and assured them of my love and commitment. Over the next few years, they often thanked me for my letters and told me how my words buoyed their spirits.

I'm still too reliant on others' affirmation. In retrospect, I see how emotionally fragile my reaction was to the time they didn't acknowledge my birthday. During a depressive episode, I'm among the sufferers who are hypersensitive and overreact to things. I also realized that only the Lord can meet my deep-seated need for love and identity. Due to fallenness and vulnerability, neither my emotional tank nor yours will be filled to the brim until we are with Him in heaven.

In the poem I pleaded for God to heal my deepest insecurities, to expand my capacity to love others instead of just using them to verify my own self-worth.

A remark by Joni Eareckson Tada complements my plea for healing of the heart. She also believes that the heart is where change begins; from it flows the refreshing stream of godly, less selfish attitudes and behaviors. After explaining how her disability resulted in much greater intimacy with God, in *Beside Bethesda: 31 Days Toward Deeper Healing,* she wrote, "God's highest priority is not our comfort or temporary prosperity, but the healing of our sin-damaged soul."[1]

? Probes to Ponder

Skim the poem again. Which lyrics resonate most with you? Why?

Does your love for anyone hinge on whether he or she meets your need for attention or affection? If so, ask God for the capacity to love that person unconditionally.

Prayer Response

Holy Spirit, keep reminding me of what the Bible says about my identity and personal security. Keep instilling in me a keen awareness that my significance isn't rooted in what I do; rather, it's based on what Christ did for me on the cross. Keep telling me that my value stems not from **who I am**, *but* **whose I am**. *Keep healing me within so I love others less selfishly and serve the gospel with purer motives. Please, don't let my fragile ego get in the way of loving others unconditionally. In the name of the One who loves me not if . . . not because . . .but in spite of, amen.*

A Pertinent Word

Jesus' words to His disciples followed a ministry trip during which they had exercised miraculous authority that He had delegated to them. Jesus looked ahead to His impending death on the cross, indicating that what He would accomplish there for them—not what they did for Him—was the basis for their identity and significance:

Nevertheless, do not rejoice in this, that the spirits are subject to you, but rejoice that your names are written in heaven.

Luke 10:20

"" An Apt Quote

Maurice Wagner's book from which I hoisted the following excerpts is the best I've ever read on the relational consequences of low self-esteem and emotional fragility. His words may resonate with you, too.

> A person deprived of love relationships in childhood is locked into a narcissistic, self-centered, self-congratulatory mode of thinking. He has to use his environment to verify himself either subtly or openly. If he cannot find sufficient verification from the admiration of others or from their envious attitudes toward him, he will invert his thinking and criticize himself, pity himself, and complain about his helplessness, or find a sense of being somebody by the help-lessness of the debilitation it causes.
>
> In wanting to be liked, we focus our attention primarily on ourselves and how we are impressing the other person. We are not really thinking of the other person's needs or his value as a person. Momentarily we acknowledge his virtues and express an admiration, but often those gratuities are in the service of needing to receive approval ourselves. We are seeking self-verification by being friendly.
>
> We need to overcome the tendency to try to relate to others for self-verification for our sense of self-identity. When we

exercise faith in God through Jesus Christ, we no longer need self-verification; we are validated. We trust in the promises of God as our security. He took our sense of being a nobody into Himself when He died for us. He became a nonentity, a nobody for us, when He died on that cross. All our own efforts at self-verification are canceled.[2]

—Maurice Wagner, *The Sensation of Being Somebody*

TWENTY-ONE

HOW DOES GOD FLESH OUT HIS LOVE?

Incarnation

The load is heavy; my body is bent.
My spirit, too, is weak and spent.
Darkness hovers, though the sun is high.
Too tired to pray; too numb to cry.

Feeling hopeless; on a downward slide.
Then you knock and come alongside.
Encouraging words, a listening ear.
I'm reassured that Christ is near.

When pain turns the heart to stone,
no one should have to go it alone.
In time and space, through thick and thin,
God wraps His love in human skin.

———

Timely Interventions

I wrote the poem for two friends who intervened to support me during a depressive episode. My wife thought I was suicidal. She called two men: my pastor and a friend who served on a different church staff.

The incarnation of Jesus refers to His birth, the embodiment of God in human form. But there's another way in which God physically demonstrates His love. Incarnation is far more than a first-century phenomenon. He also gift-wraps His love in the form of other people in the body of Christ.

My pastor took me to breakfast, reassured me of his love, prayed for me and pleaded with me to seek medical intervention due to the chronic nature of my depression. I had never consulted a physician or considered medicine for it. I falsely assumed that more faith was all I needed.

I heeded his counsel. For several years, an antidepressant alleviated the harshest symptoms.

The other friend showed up unexpectedly at my house that evening, the same day I met my pastor for breakfast. He announced, "I hear you've had a few rough days. I don't come with advice, but you need to know that I'm here for you. If you want to talk and pray, I'm available. But even if you'd rather read or watch TV, I'm not leaving your side for the next two hours!"

More than a decade after those interventions, over lunch at my university, a different friend saw my tears and sad countenance, evidence of yet another descent into despondency.

After I returned to my office, where I lay in a fetal position, totally immobilized, he came by unexpectedly. He couldn't concentrate on work back in his office due to his concern for me. He wept and said, "I don't know what to say to help you, but I'm here." Then he prayed for me on the spot.

His presence spoke louder than any words he could have used.

Coming Alongside

Those three friends physically came alongside me. The Greek verb translated "to encourage" literally means, "to come alongside."

Do you recall the last time you couldn't start your car due to a dead battery? You asked someone to pull his car alongside yours. He employed jumper cables to connect his good battery with your depleted one. When he started his car, energy flowed from his working battery and replenished your weaker battery until it functioned on its own.

What a picture of the ministry of encouragement! It occurs when sensitive people come alongside a hurting person and provide an infusion of strength. How grateful I am for the friends who gave me a jump!

Not Meant to Go It Alone

Perhaps you don't identify with my mental illness, yet you experience times when you can't manage things alone, when you need the presence of and input from others.

When you lose your job. When you face a scary health challenge. When you're discouraged over relational conflicts in your family. When you need input for a crucial decision. When a child or grandchild is born with a birth defect. When you need a brother or sister in Christ to hold you accountable and pray for you during a time of complacency in your walk with Christ.

The New Testament contains over 60 commands that show God's intent for relationships among Christians. 1 Thessalonians 5:11 adequately captures my friends' effect on me: "Encourage one another and build one another up."

God's primary means of loving us remains incarnational. Yet no one can help us bear a burden unless we're willing to swallow our pride, to let the other person know we're hurting, to risk appearing as if we aren't living victoriously. (Then again, perhaps we *are* living victoriously when we tap into one of God's intended means of support!)

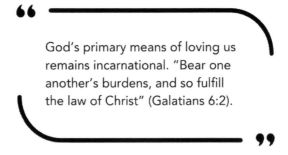

God's primary means of loving us remains incarnational. "Bear one another's burdens, and so fulfill the law of Christ" (Galatians 6:2).

Remember: when you think God has abandoned you in a time of suffering, He often shows up in the form of others in the body of Christ. "Bear one another's burdens, and so fulfill the law of Christ" (Galatians 6:2).

? Probes to Ponder

Think of an occasion when another Christian ministered to you or met a need of yours in some way. Did you thank the Lord for loving you through this person?

Is a current need or stressor weighing you down, yet you haven't disclosed it to anyone because you fear it will reflect poorly on you? How long will you allow pride to prevent you from receiving the help Christ has for you in the form of other people?

Do you know anyone in your sphere of influence who has a need that you can help meet? What will you do or say to come alongside this person and give him or her a jump?

Prayer Response

Father, forgive me for all the times I've suffered alone because I wouldn't own up to the depth of my despair. Help me to stop worrying so much about my reputation and what others think of me, to shuck my pride which robs my friends of a ministry You prepared for them. Remind me that when I refuse their help through my silence, I'm also refusing Your assistance. In the name of One who called me both a friend (John 15:15) and a brother (Hebrews 2:11-12), amen.

◆ A Pertinent Word

Blessed be the God and Father of our Lord Jesus Christ, the Father of mercies and God of all comfort, who comforts us in all our affliction, so that we may be able to comfort those who are in any affliction, with the comfort with which we ourselves are comforted by God.

2 Corinthians 1:3-4

An Apt Quote

Friends are those rare people who ask how we are and then wait to hear the answer.[1]

—Ed Cunningham

TWENTY-TWO
WHY DO YOU NEED OTHER CHRISTIANS?

Gracious Gifts

Gifts nestled under limbs, basking in lights' glow.
We listen to Christmas hymns on disk or radio.
Clothed in red or green or gold; proud of perfect bow.
Presents someone sold us with a jolly "Ho-Ho-Ho."

Pick one up. Feel its weight. Shake the box and guess.
On Christmas morning its fate is to surprise and bless.
Fingers poking in each box; the floor a cheery mess.
The candle-scented house rocks. Warm hearts whisper, "Yes!"

Yet far more precious gifts come wrapped in human skin.
Their companionship uplifts. They are blood-bought kin.
Their presence instills cheer as we lounge in the den.
Not unwrapped once a year: they're ours through thick and thin.

Purchased not with cards or cash, these items do not break.
There won't be a gift exchange; our choice was no mistake.

Not like a toy, or clothes we wear, their worth can't be measured.
A lifetime warranty is there. Forever, they'll be treasured.

Friends: A Means of Grace

I gave this "Gracious Gifts" poem to a dear couple when our families celebrated Christmas together. As I illustrated in the previous chapter, God incarnates His love through other Christians who He brings into our lives. Through shared experiences and mutual ministry, close friends serve as a conduit through which God sends His sustaining grace.

David and Esther, recipients of the poem, became good friends when we served together on a large church staff. We shared lots of meals, prayed together and sharpened each other as we discussed church issues and principles. After 18 years of geographical separation, they moved to our area. Our companionship picked up once again.

I know what it's like to be so distraught over a relational conflict at work that I knocked on their door and said, through tears, "Esther, can I borrow David for a while?" I desperately needed his intercession and counsel. I recall how they paid for a plane ticket that I couldn't afford so I could visit my dying dad in an out-of-state hospital. And they, like the three men I mentioned in the previous chapter, accepted me and ministered to me during times of despondency and emotional fragility. Though our ministry to each other was mutual, their friendship strengthened and stabilized me on multiple occasions.

I think of the authentic fellowship we experienced with them when I reflect on "Redwood Theology."

What Is Redwood Theology?

The closer they are to one another, the more they thrive, the better they grow. The togetherness they experience enables each one to withstand the inevitable assaults of adversaries. When threatening circumstances encroach, they support one another. Their individual health depends on nutrients others provide.

I'm referring to the largest, most enduring living things on earth: *Giant sequoia trees* (also called "Redwoods").

It isn't unusual for a sequoia tree to live 2,000 years. A few have reached a height of 350 feet, the equivalent of a 30-story building. At least one redwood grew 25 feet in diameter. They grow better in close-knit groves. When these trees drop cones, twigs and bark, the subsequent decomposition by the soil's organisms keep returning nutrients to the soil, enabling the trees to keep growing even when rainfall is low.

The second reason they grow better in groves impresses me more. You might conclude that trees this big force their roots deeply into the earth. How else can they survive and stand ramrod straight when high winds and other forces of nature assail them?

That isn't the case, though. Redwoods burrow anywhere from three to twelve feet down, not deep enough to support the weight of such monster trees.[1]

What is their secret?

Interdependence.

Partnership.

Community.

Redwoods demonstrate the equivalent of what Christians call "authentic fellowship." Instead of anchoring their roots far down, their roots spread horizontally far from the trunk—occasionally as far as 100 yards! When the trees grow close together, their roots intertwine, wrapping around each other. By interlocking with the roots of several nearby trees, any given tree is much stronger, more stable, than it would be on its own.

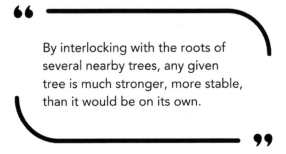

> By interlocking with the roots of several nearby trees, any given tree is much stronger, more stable, than it would be on its own.

What a picture of the necessity of close relationships among God's people, especially when stormy circumstances threaten our spiritual and emotional equilibrium!

Supporting One Another

Referring to members of the body of Christ, Paul wrote, "If one member suffers, all suffer together; if one member is honored, all rejoice together. Now you are the body of Christ and individually members of it" (1 Corinthians 12:26-27). Scores of relational commands in the New Testament reveal our need for each other, such as "bear one another's burdens" (Galatians 6:2); "show hospitality to one another" (1 Peter 4:9); "stir up one another to love and good deeds" (Hebrews 10:24); "teaching and admonishing one another" (Colossians 3:16), and "forgiving one another" (Ephesians 4:32).

When discouragement or a setback occurs, let's intertwine with others so we're strong enough to withstand whatever threatens our stability and growth in the Lord. What can we do so our feeble roots don't try to bear all the weight that's causing our spirits to sag? Ask God for root-entwining friends, then take the initiative to serve others in their time of need. The more love and support you give, the more you'll receive. Wrap your roots around others when they're in need and the Lord will nudge some of those folks to wrap their roots around yours in return.

That's what David and Esther did for us, and what we did for them.

Now I'll shift the focus away from close friends to someone else you may need to wrap your roots around. This person may never become a good friend, but he or she could still serve as a gracious gift from God.

I'm referring to a personal counselor or therapist.

The Value of a Counselor

The counselor I've visited most frequently is a devout Christian with an advanced degree in psychology. He sees everything through the lens of a biblical worldview. What he knows about human thought processes and behavior enables him to listen intelligently, to offer insights on the triggers for and relational implications of a major depressive episode.

Tom didn't cure my depression, but he helped me to manage it. Gradually, things he said and questions he posed seeped into the creases of my mind and made sense, affecting how I responded to people and to circumstances.

When I broached painful memories, I asked him why I still hurt even though I had forgiven the parties who had sinned against me. He pointed out that emotional scars remain, even decades after a traumatic experience of rejection or conflict. He explained that the forgiveness we extend may dissolve resentment but doesn't necessarily erase the pain. He revealed reasons in my background for what I called my "neediness" (excessive reliance on others' affection). Yet he nudged me to love others unconditionally when they don't return the same degree of affection that I demonstrated toward them. "The past still affects you," he declared, "yet it doesn't have to control you."

Tom also beamed a ray of light on the correlation between a melancholy mood and temptation. Though he asserted that sin didn't directly cause my depression, he said that I'm more vulnerable to certain sins, especially those of the flesh, when I'm downcast. He worked with me to identify situations and stressors that hurled me closer to the abyss of depression, or which ramped up temptation when I'm mired in a bog of despondency. He insisted that certain temptations promise, falsely, an escape from the pain.

He served as a means of God's grace to me.

Cooperating with Your Counselor

The reason you need a counselor probably differs from mine.

You may need a Christian counselor to help you deal with painful memories. To help you salvage a troubled marriage. To coach you in forgiving a perpetrator of abuse. To guide you in striving to reconcile with an estranged grown child or deal with an autistic child. To assist you in overcoming an addiction.

When you seek a counselor to wrap your roots around, though his or her credentials and experience are crucial factors, whether you receive the needed help may depend more on you. A redwood tree doesn't just stand there. The tree must reach out and extend its roots before other trees' roots can grab them.

Apply these tips I've learned from scores of counseling sessions.

- *Be brutally honest and transparent with your counselor.*
  Don't withhold anything from your story or worry
  about whether he or she will disrespect you if you
  spill the unvarnished truth. Don't waste time and
  money pretending you're more spiritual and mature
  than you are. Disclose past traumas, relational
  disputes, sin patterns—anything that shows how you

tick or why you don't. If pride keeps you from doing this, counseling won't help. No one can help bear your burdens if you don't reveal those burdens.

- *Approach counseling like you would a course with an esteemed professor.* Prepare as if you'll be tested on the sessions. Take notes of the interactions. Review those notes before the next session, then jot down questions to ask the counselor next time. Your questions should seek clarification of something the counselor said or get the counselor's take on a new subject.

Through a competent Christian counselor, God may heal your *heart,* purifying your affections and motives, and help heal your *mind,* shaping how you think about what happens to you. The prerequisite for receiving help is extending your roots horizontally, trusting another person to interlock with you, to fuel your growth.

God created each of us with missing parts. We find those parts that complete us in the form of close friends in the body of Christ, and sometimes through a wise Christian counselor. When we can't manage life on our own, we see that Jesus' death on the cross blessed us with blood-bought kin through whom He loves us.

? Probes to Ponder

Do you have someone whose companionship instills joy and strengthens you in times of need?

If so, handwrite this gift from God a note beginning with these words: "I thank God for you because _____," then fill in the blanks. If not, ask Him to bring such a person into the inner circle of your life.

Can you think of someone in your circle of relationships who needs the stability that your love could provide? What can you say to or do for this person to start wrapping your roots around his or hers?

Are you experiencing a problem or circumstance that needs the insight a counselor could provide? Ask your pastor or someone else you trust to recommend someone whose expertise and experience matches your area of need.

 Prayer Response

Jesus, thank You for calling Your followers "friends" (John 15:15). And thank You for other friends through whom You love and support me. May I serve others as lavishly as my closest friends and counselors have served me. In Your precious name, amen.

 A Pertinent Word

A friend loves at all times, and a brother is born for adversity.

Proverbs 17:17

99   An Apt Quote

Fellowship means that we are ready to receive Christ from others. Other believers minister Christ to us, and we are ready to receive. [2]

—Watchman Nee

TWENTY-THREE

WHAT IS THE MOST IMPORTANT SERMON YOU WILL EVER HEAR?

Telling Yourself the Truth

*When all hope yields to despair
and I doubt that God is there;
when my heart is cold, unfeeling,
and my prayers bounce off the ceiling;
when depression takes its toll
and winter winds assault my soul;
when I totter due to pain;
cry for relief, but in vain;
when relationships turn sour;
when my attitude is dour;
when the race seems all uphill
and dying grows in its appeal,
which lens am I looking through?
It's what God says that is true.
When things don't go as expected,
still, His truth is unaffected.*

When Satan says, "God does not care!"
I see the cross: Christ's blood stains there.
When I'm tempted by what is wrong,
God's promises of help prove strong.
When guilt nags and I'm overwhelmed,
His Word insists, "You aren't condemned!"
When I fear taking my last breath,
Christ asserts, "I defeated death!"
When my body throbs with piercing pain,
He reminds me of the new one I'll gain.
When my heart breaks and tears outpour,
He says, "One day you'll weep no more!"
When false beliefs vie for control,
preaching God's Word strengthens my soul.
When Satan whispers, I reply
with God's Word to refute the lie.

A Realistic Perspective

In the poem, I begin by acknowledging that the road on which we walk with Christ is often pockmarked by difficulties and uphill treks that exhaust us. The lyrics cite tests of faith such as temperamental weaknesses, bodily pain, doubt, unanswered prayer, relationship conflicts, vulnerability to sin and Satan's lies. No wonder Paul told Timothy to "fight the good fight of the faith" (1 Timothy 6:12). Though our earthly pilgrimage teems with divine blessings that bring happiness, we must not expect on earth what God only promised for heaven: a trouble-free life.

The second stanza illustrates a means of fighting: *talking back to the false beliefs we tell ourselves and combating the lies of Satan with truths in God's written Word.* I call this practice "preaching to myself." One way I preach to myself is through poetry I write. More often, I literally talk to myself—sometimes out loud!

This spiritual discipline or habit is indispensable to my faith. Though we desperately need the biblical sermons delivered weekly by our pastors, I'm convinced of a key insight pertaining to the power of sermons. This conviction permeates my heart, soul and mind. It's the most life-changing concept I've experienced this side of the cross.

The most sin-defeating, hope-instilling, faith-sustaining, soul-nourishing, ministry-motivating sermons you'll ever hear are the ones you preach to yourself!

> The most sin-defeating, hope-instilling, faith-sustaining, soul-nourishing, ministry-motivating sermons you'll ever hear are the ones you preach to yourself!

What Is "Preaching to Yourself?"

"Preaching to yourself" is the assertive act of combating discouragement, temptation and any other harmful thought pattern with the truth of God's Word. It's giving a biblically informed rebuttal to erroneous or distorted thinking, including the lies that Satan whispers to us. What and how a Christ-follower thinks, how he "talks to himself" and whether he refutes misconceptions and false conclusions, affect spiritual vitality and usefulness to God.

Is Preaching to Yourself Biblical?

Without a doubt!

One of the sons of Korah talked back to depression by pointing himself to a brighter future stemming from faith in God: "Why are you cast down, O my soul, and why are you in turmoil within me? Hope in God; for I shall again praise him, my salvation" (Psalm 42:5).

In a psalm prompted by an experience of treachery and opposition, David addressed himself concerning God's character: "For God alone, O my soul, wait in silence, for my hope is from him. He only is my rock and my salvation, my fortress; I shall not be shaken" (Psalm 62:5-6).

In Psalm 73:26, Asaph, after acknowledging his own weakness and failure, reminded himself that God is his source of strength: "My flesh and my heart may fail, but God is the strength of my heart and my portion forever."

Though many psalms were written as prayers to God, or lyrics to sing during corporate worship, the samples I gave show three different authors preaching to themselves. In their time of need, they focused on God: who He is, what He has done and what He has pledged to do for His people. We, too, must fight discouragement, temptations and negative thoughts that roil around in our minds by continually reminding ourselves of the promises and truths in Scripture.

A prerequisite for effectively "preaching to ourselves" is consistent time delving into God's Word. Memorizing key verses or longer passages prepares us for such preaching. I've memorized scores of Bible texts over the years. Hiding God's Word in my heart allows me to retrieve His truth at the precise moment I need it, giving the Holy Spirit fuel to work with in my mind.

Rich Bible Texts for Preaching to Yourself

Use the following felt needs and related texts as catalysts for your thinking concerning when and what to preach to yourself. These examples will enable you to refute false beliefs and harmful feelings.

Preach to yourself when...

- *You don't feel God's presence*: Isaiah 41:10; Matthew 28:20; John 14:16; Hebrews 13:5
- *You don't believe you can keep overcoming a particular temptation:* 1 John 4:4; 1 Corinthians 10:13; 2 Thessalonians 3:3
- *You're experiencing uncertainty or delay*: Psalm 27:13-14; Psalm 62:5-8
- *You're in a dark depressive episode*: Micah 7:8; Psalm 42; Psalm 54:4
- *You tell yourself that things are hopeless*: Lamentations 3:22-25; Romans 15:13

- *You feel fearful or threatened by things like terrorism or pandemics*: Psalm 46:1-2, 10; Psalm 56:3-4
- *You doubt God's goodness:* Nahum 1:7; Isaiah 30:18
- *Satan whispers that God is angry at you over past sins*: Romans 5:1-2; Romans 8:1; 1 John 2:1-2
- *The burden you're bearing is about to break you:* Psalm 55:22; Psalm 68:19; Matthew 11:28-30
- *You browbeat yourself over weaknesses or mistakes:* Psalm 73:25-26; 1 Corinthians 1:26-29; 2 Corinthians 4:7
- *Your heart breaks and you aren't sure that God cares*: Psalm 30:5; Psalm 34:18-19; Psalm 147:3; Zephaniah 3:17
- *You tell yourself that you can't succeed in a task or ministry to which God has called you:* 1 Corinthians 15:58; 2 Corinthians 3:5-6
- *You look at the frightening world situation and start doubting if God is actually in control:* Ephesians 1:11; Psalm 103:19
- *You're retired, you feel unsettled, even scared of what the future may hold:* Psalm 71:9, 17-21

God's Word generates the faith needed to function in our fallen world: "So faith comes by hearing, and hearing by the word of Christ" (Romans 10:17). Memorizing God's Word, then preaching it to yourself, isn't a panacea that eliminates pain, spiritual warfare, temperamental frailties or adverse circumstances. Yet God's truth will strengthen you, resulting in more victories than you would otherwise experience.

Now I'll explore in more detail the internal battle for belief that accompanies preaching to yourself.

A Battle for Belief

Day in and day out, there's a battlefield in our mind where spiritual warfare occurs. It's a battle of belief. Will we trust in fragile, vacillating feelings and destructive thoughts, or will we rely, in desperation, on the truths in God's Word? Who or what will we choose to believe? What is the source of authority on which we will stake our life and daily choices: subjective feelings, pessimistic thoughts, or God's objective truth?

Truth is objective and external to us. We don't create it. The discouraging and erroneous things we feel and tell ourselves are subjective ruminations of fallen creatures. When the body throbs in pain or the spirit is downcast, we can't trust what we think or feel. Yet we *can* trust God's absolute truth!

God's truth never changes. His truth just is! That's the perspective that generated the poem.

? Probes to Ponder

What lies does the enemy of your soul most often whisper to you?

When you're discouraged, hurt or on the verge of yielding to temptation, what falsehoods do you sometimes tell yourself?

Examine once again the felt needs and related Bible texts in the chapter section, "Rich Bible Texts for Preaching to Yourself." Which need listed in italics describes a current condition you're facing? Will you slowly absorb the content of the corresponding verses from God's Word?

Why is the act of "preaching to yourself" *not* a superficial, glib use of God's Word?

 Prayer Response

Oh Father, how glad I am that my dark moods and discouraging circumstances don't produce my theology! Who You are and all that You promised are so much more reliable than what I think or how I feel. Instead of being dependent on my experience, Your truth informs my experience. May Your Spirit keep reminding me of precious truths in Your Word. Give me a teachable, responsive spirit when I preach Your Word to myself. In the name of Jesus, the only person who fully practiced what He preached, amen.

 A Pertinent Word

For though we walk in the flesh, we are not waging war according to the flesh. For the weapons of our warfare are not of the flesh but have divine power to destroy strongholds. We destroy arguments and every lofty opinion raised against the knowledge of God, and take every thought captive to obey Christ.

2 Corinthians 10:3-5

An Apt Quote

What follows is a summary of a podcast with Paul Tripp, titled "Preach the Gospel to Yourself."

No one is more influential in your life than you are, because no one talks to you more than you do.

In our sin, we constantly find our responses to life in our fallen world to be disconnected from the theology that we confess. Anger, fear, panic, and discouragement stalk our hearts and whisper a false gospel that will lure our lives away from what we say we believe.

The battleground is meditation. What is it that is capturing your idle thoughts? What fear or frustration is filling your spare moments?

Will you just listen to yourself, or will you start talking to yourself? No, preaching to yourself! Not letting your concerns shape you but forming your concerns by the gospel.

Preaching the gospel to ourselves is a spiritual discipline that is both proactive and reactive. It's reactive as we encounter temptation and frustration and seek to restock in the moment, or as we reflect back on our sin and circumstances and try to evaluate them with a gospel lens.

But it's also proactive—it goes on the offense—when we feed our souls in some regular rhythm before the events and tasks and disappointments of daily life begin streaming our way.

There is a difference between merely reminding ourselves of truth and preaching to ourselves the truth of the gospel. The latter is self-consciously and intentionally reminding ourselves of the person and presence and provisions of our Redeemer.

But while gospel self-preaching is not the same thing as Bible reading, the connections and interdependences are profound. The Scriptures provide the inerrant material for preaching to ourselves the gospel of grace. They are the content to be taken up and applied to our lives in view of Jesus' person and work.[1]

TWENTY-FOUR
CAN YOU RELY ON HOW YOU FEEL?

Feelings Are Not My Fuel

"I do not feel like praying,"
I told God, despite my need.
That's when He whispered, saying,
"Now that's a prayer I will heed!"

I felt no hunger for God's Word.
I digested it, anyway.
A surprising thing occurred:
my spirit felt full all day.

I felt bleak; wanted to pout.
Other folks? I wanted no part.
By faith I chose to reach out.
That is when God warmed my heart.

No passion prompted me to serve.
"Won't do any good!" I lamented.

That is when the Lord threw a curve:
that's the day someone repented.

Feelings are fickle. One minute I'm low.
The next minute, my feelings may soar.
I don't rely on them; I know
I can trust in God's Word far more.

In the previous chapter, I explained the spiritual practice of preaching God's truth to ourselves as a way to counter untrue things we tell ourselves. Now I'll expand that discussion and give more examples. The poem that launched this chapter emphasizes the reliability of God's Word, in sharp contrast to pessimistic feelings and attitudes that try to defeat us.

Feelings or Thoughts?

God created us with the wonderful capacity *to feel.*

Whether it's the unfettered joy of holding a new baby for the first time, the subtle exuberance when we accomplish a hard-won goal, the awe-inspiring appreciation for a roseate sunset or the rib-tickling laughter generated by watching a puppy at play, God blessed us with the gracious gift of feeling.

But we experience feelings on the negative side of the spectrum, too.

Sometimes we battle discouragement, hopelessness, fear, anger, worry and insecurity.

There's a strong connection between *how we feel* and *what we think.* Sometimes, what we label "feelings" are instead "thoughts or beliefs" that control us. For example, when I say that I *feel* depressed, I'm actually in the vise-grip of pessimistic and oppressive thoughts. That's why experts call severe, recurring depression a *mental* illness. That mental state then generates negative feelings, such as sadness or anxiety.

It's often difficult to distinguish between a thought (a judgment, belief, opinion or perspective) and a feeling or emotion. Yet many psychologists believe that how or what we think generates feelings. (The thought of visiting a new grandchild generates a feeling of delight or happiness. A person who lost his job to budget cutbacks believes he won't find a new position in his field; the consequence may be anger or despair.)

The spiritual practice of preaching to ourselves involves talking back to inner states that drag us down and don't align with the truth of God's Word. Whether the phenomenon we're opposing is a false belief (thought) or a defeatist feeling is, in one sense, a matter of semantics.

> 66
>
> The spiritual practice of preaching to ourselves involves talking back to inner states that drag us down and don't align with the truth of God's Word.
>
> 99

Feelings and False Beliefs Versus Truth

Now I'll *show* you three concrete examples of countering false beliefs and the negative emotional states those mindsets create. Even if you don't identify with all three areas of need I cite, reading these illustrations will better prepare you to preach God's Word to yourself.

Handling Discouragement about Ministry

When I'm disheartened over a lack of visible results, I don't *think* a Bible teaching responsibility is worth the time and effort it requires. I may not *feel* excited or motivated. When discouragement over teaching or preaching takes over, I talk back to it with what God says about His revelation of truth, which we have in the Bible.

Jeremiah 23:29

"Is not my word like fire, declares the Lord, and like a hammer that breaks the rock in pieces?"

John 8:31-32

"If you abide in my words, you are truly my disciples, and you will know the truth, and the truth will set you free."

Hebrews 4:12

"For the word of God is living and active, sharper than any two-edged sword, piercing to the division of soul and of spirit, of joints and marrow, and discerning the thoughts and intents of the heart."

I remind myself that the efficacy of communicating God's Word relies less on my giftedness, experience and delivery than it does with the innate power of God's Word and the Holy Spirit's work in reaching folks' hearts with God's truth. I don't stay downcast because I remember that I'm merely a conduit through which His Word and Spirit flow. Only *He* can funnel truth from a learner's head to his heart, so I pray for Him to do what only He can do.

When my concentration is on my limitations and spiritual inconsistency, I may mumble that God can't keep using someone like me. That's when I preach to myself God's words to Paul, who felt that a "thorn in the flesh" hindered his service: "My grace is sufficient for you, for my power is made perfect in weakness" (2 Corinthians 12:9). Then I reply as Paul did: "Therefore I will boast all the more gladly of my weaknesses, so that the power of Christ may rest on me. For the sake of Christ, then, I am content with weaknesses, insults, hardships, persecutions, and calamities. For when I am weak, then I am strong" (vs. 9-10).

It's all about *Him*, not me.

Fighting Strong Temptations

A lie the enemy often tells me is that I can't defeat a particular temptation. He reminds me of all the times I've fallen and, in effect, says, "Give up, Terry. You can't resist this forever. Aren't you weary of this relentless barrage? After all, your Bible says God will forgive you. What will it hurt to give in? Relieve the pressure—it will feel so good!"

That's when verses I've memorized scroll across the screen of my mind.

1 Corinthians 10:13

"God is faithful, and he will not let you be tempted beyond your ability, but with the temptation he will also provide the way of escape, that you may be able to endure it."

2 Thessalonians 3:3

"But the Lord is faithful. He will establish you and guard you against the evil one."

2 Corinthians 10:3-4

"For though we walk in the flesh, we are not waging war according to the flesh. For the weapons of our warfare are not of the flesh but have divine power to destroy strongholds."

Before I remind myself of those promises, I feel extremely vulnerable and spiritually frail. I'm on the cusp of giving in and falling into the abyss of disobedience. But after reviewing those verses, I say this to the Lord:

> Father, either your power working in me is stronger than this lure, or those Bible promises are flat-out lies! I choose to believe they're true. Please, for the sake of Your glory in and through my life, strengthen me right now so I don't grieve You with sin. By grace you saved me from the eternal penalty for sin, and now, by grace, keep me from practicing sin. Thank You for encouraging me to come to You when I'm needy. Your Word says, "Let us then with confidence draw near to the throne of grace, that we may receive mercy and find grace to help in time of need" (Hebrews 4:16).

Responding to Discouragement

When I fall into the abyss of discouragement, that's when false beliefs most viciously vie for my attention. I tell myself lies that keep me from reveling in the gospel and which thwart motivation for ministry. I *know* better in the cognitive realm, yet what I say I believe doesn't always seep into the realm of emotions—not when a dark mood envelops me. When I'm despondent, the typical stressors and setbacks that everyone experiences trigger an almost endless cycle of oppressive thoughts and feelings. I'm more prone to mutter this to myself: "Why do I keep fighting against despondency? Despair always returns. I'll never be happy again!"

To combat such hopelessness, I quote the following Bible verses to myself and plead with God to instill more joy and hope within me:

Psalm 42:11

"Why are you cast down, O my soul, and why are you in turmoil within me? Hope in God; for I shall again praise him, my salvation and my God."

Micah 7:8

"Rejoice not over me, O my enemy; when I fall, I shall rise; when I sit in darkness, the Lord will be a light to me."

Psalm 50:15

"And call upon me in the day of trouble; I will deliver you, and you shall glorify me."

In Psalm 50:15, there's a direct grammatical link between calling on God in times of trouble, and the promise that God will receive glory through His answer. I plead, "Father, strengthen me in this time of weakness. Assuage this hopelessness so that I teach, write and relate to people in a way that honors You. Though people may view me as weak, may they see You as strong and capable by how you sustain and use me."

Daily Warfare

Day in and day out, it's imperative to preach the gospel to yourself, to review truths in God's Word that counteract falsehoods concocted by distorted thinking and oppressive feelings. Preaching to yourself must occur daily because spiritual warfare happens daily. Just as hungry lions hunt for prey daily, so does Satan: "Be sober minded; be watchful. Your adversary the devil prowls around like a roaring lion, seeking someone to devour" (1 Peter 5:8).

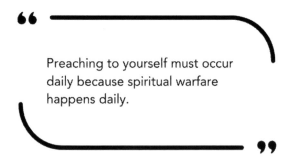

> Preaching to yourself must occur daily because spiritual warfare happens daily.

This spiritual practice of preaching to myself doesn't keep me sinless, but it's something I do that empowers me to sin less. It doesn't mean that unfavorable feelings or attitudes never characterize me, but the discipline shortens my stay on the unfavorable side of the feeling spectrum.

Funneling God's truth into my mind helps to dispel negative thought patterns and oppressive feelings so they don't constantly reign in my mind and heart.

? Probes to Ponder

You read three examples from my life of preaching to myself: when discouraged about ministry; when pommeled by temptation and when caught in the vise-grip of discouragement. Which of these areas of need resonate most with you? How do those examples help you grasp how to preach to yourself when a false belief or oppressive feeling tries to dominate your life?

What action or discipline on your part best prepares you to "preach to yourself" effectively?

Prayer Response

Father, thank You for teaching me that I can't trust all my feelings, and for showing me through experience that I can trust what You say in Your Word. Focusing on Your written Word won't eliminate all harmful emotions and troubling mindsets, but it will help me to sort out what is true and what is not. In the name of Your Son, who embodied truth (John 14:6) and who declared, "Your Word is truth" (John 17:17), amen.

A Pertinent Word

We also thank God constantly for this, that when you received the word of God, which you heard from us, you accepted it not as the word of men, but as what it really is, the word of God, which is at work in you believers.

1 Thessalonians 2:13

An Apt Quote

Within the Scripture there is a balm for every wound, a salve for every sore.[1]

—Charles Spurgeon

TWENTY-FIVE

DO YOU FEEL HOPELESS?

Hopeless?

Fleeting, it's like a bird in flight,
or like a shooting star at night,
or lightning that spans the sky.
Gone in the blink of an eye.

Elusive, like the fog that lifts
when morning sun sends its gifts;
or the zigzagging butterfly
that you can't catch; no use to try.

That's my relationship to hope.
It's like a wet bar of soap
that keeps giving me the slip.
Can't keep it within my grip.

Hope that a blazing beam of light
will penetrate my soul's dark night.

Hope that it will not seem strange
that how I think and feel will change.

Can God plant hope within a heart
for peace of mind and a fresh start?
Though right now I am without it,
God shouts "Yes!" Should I doubt it?

"Why are you cast down, O my soul,
and why are you in turmoil within me?
Hope in God; for I shall again praise him,
My salvation and my God" (Psalm 42:5).

———

When I'm caught in the vise grip of depression, hopelessness aptly describes me. Negative thinking typically complements a dark mood. The poem realistically depicts a hopeless mind-set, but I end on a positive note. In yet another example of "preaching to myself," I finished the poem with a Bible verse in which the author talked back to his despair and exalts God as the object and giver of hope.

Hope rooted in the gospel of Christ and the benefits of His death on the cross is essential for every believer, not just to those of us who are depression-prone.

The Bible and Hope

We tend to employ the term "hope" as a mere wish: either one that has little chance of materializing, or an outcome that we honestly don't expect to happen. (We *hope* our assigned number in the Publisher's Clearing House sweepstakes wins the $5 million-dollar prize. Or we *hope* the expected rain doesn't wipe out our child's baseball game.)

But in the Bible, *hope* is far more than merely a yearning or a hankering after something. The most common Old Testament word translated hope refers to a strong expectation, associated with *trusting in* or *waiting on* God. Similarly, in the New Testament, the primary Greek term translated hope is a confident expectation rooted in the gospel of Jesus Christ and its promise of eternal life. For believers, hope isn't based on random chance or a long-shot occurrence, but on a Person!

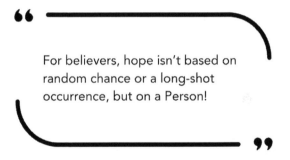

> For believers, hope isn't based on random chance or a long-shot occurrence, but on a Person!

What distinguishes hope from a mere wish is the objective source of hope: *God.* Our hope deepens as we learn more about Him and His attributes. The more we focus on Him, instead of ourselves and the amount of faith we have or don't have, the more our faith and hope increase. Hope seeps into us when we see the cross of Christ clearly and identify what His death accomplished for us.

Mull over this small sampling of Bible verses and the insights they offer.

- *The foundation of a Christian's hope is a Person: either God the Father or Jesus Christ, His Son.* "For God alone, O my soul, wait in silence, for my hope is from him" (Psalm 62:5). Paul summarized the mystery of the gospel as "Christ in you, the hope of glory" (Colossians 1:27).
- *Hope in the Lord and the gospel provides an impetus for ministry.* Referring to his efforts to spread the gospel, Paul wrote, "To this end we toil and strive, because we have our hope set on the living God" (1 Timothy 4:10).
- *God's Word links hope to the attributes of God's unfailing love and faithfulness.* "The steadfast love of the Lord never ceases; his mercies never come to an end; they are new every morning; great is your faithfulness. 'The Lord is my portion,' says my soul, 'therefore I will hope in him'" (Lamentations 3:22-24).
- *Hope in the gospel not only sustains us during trials, but stronger hope may be the outcome of suffering.* "We rejoice in our sufferings, knowing that suffering produces endurance, and endurance produces character, and character produces hope" (Romans 5:4).
- *Exercising hope in the Lord never lets us down due to the Holy Spirit's work within us.* "Hope does not disappoint, because the love of God has been poured out within our hearts through the Holy Spirit who was given to us" (Romans 5:5, NASB).
- *Knowing the truths in God's Word kindles hope within us.* "Whatever was written in former days was written for our instruction, that through endurance

and through the encouragement of the Scriptures we might have hope" (Romans 15:4).

- *A Christian's hope isn't a flimsy wish or fantasy, but a confident assurance associated with virile faith.* "Now faith is the assurance of things hoped for, the conviction of things not seen" (Hebrews 11:1).
- *Hope in the second coming of Christ purifies us during our earthly pilgrimage.* "Beloved, we are God's children now, and what we will be has not yet appeared; but we know that when he appears we shall be like him, because we shall see him as he is. And everyone who thus hopes in him purifies himself as he is pure" (1 John 3:3).
- *Our capacity to hope is a grace gift from God.* "May our Lord Jesus Christ himself, and God our Father, who loved us and gave us eternal comfort and good hope through grace, comfort your hearts and establish them in every good work and word" (2 Thessalonians 2:16).
- *Remembering God's promises instills hope within us.* The basis for Abraham's hope for an heir stemmed from God's repeated promise of an heir (Genesis 12:1-3, 13:16; 15:5-6). According to Romans 4:18, "In hope he believed against hope, that he should become the father of many nations, as he had been told."
- *As Christians, hope isn't something we potentially possess. It's a gift that is real and constant, since it's embodied in Jesus Christ. Yet we often have a vision problem and don't see our hope (or Him) clearly. And for that, there's enlightening grace!* Paul prayed that the Ephesians would have "the eyes of your heart

enlightened, that you may know what is the hope to which he has called you, what are the riches of his glorious inheritance in the saints" (Ephesians 1:18-19).

No wonder R. C. Sproul said this about hope: "Hope is called the anchor of the soul (Hebrews 6:19), because it gives stability to the Christian life. But hope is not simply a 'wish' (I wish that such-and-such would take place); rather, it is that which latches on to the certainty of the promises of the future that God has made."[1]

? Probes to Ponder

If someone asked you to summarize one insight about hope offered by this chapter, what would you say?

Which insight from the previous Bible references resonates most with you today? Why?

What causes hopelessness to settle in your heart or mind?

- An unanswered prayer concerning a burden that's weighing you down?
- Relentless temptations that weaken your resistance?
- Estrangement from a loved one that continues, despite repeated efforts to reconcile?
- Physical pain or an illness that medical intervention doesn't alleviate?

Ask the Lord for the grace gift of hope to sustain you during this difficult time.

Prayer Response

Adapt the words and elements of this prayer so it conveys your unique situation:

Holy Spirit, when hopelessness or pessimistic thinking envelops me, please counter it by reminding me of all that You, God the Father and God the Son have done for me. Stir up gratitude within me for my wife of over 50 years; for my two grown sons; my daughter-in-law and grandson, and for the close friends who know me well—yet somehow still love me! Remind me that this aging body will someday stop aching and it will become imperishable (1 Corinthians 15:42-43). Turn my mind to the reality that despair won't stalk me in the new heaven and the new earth. Tears, pain, mourning and death won't siphon off joy there (Revelation 21:4). Oh, please, instill hope rooted in Your faithful promises. And on those days here and now, when my faith is in short supply, remind me that the Object of my faith is unlimited in strength and power. In the name of Jesus, whose sacrificial death on the cross and subsequent resurrection provide an objective, historical basis for my hope, amen.

A Pertinent Word

May the God of hope fill you with all joy and peace in believing, so that by the power of the Holy Spirit you may abound in hope.

Romans 15:13

👄 An Apt Quote

Here is the radical truth of the gospel. Hope is not a situation. Hope is not a location. Hope is not a possession. Hope is not an experience. Hope is more than an insight or a truism. Hope is a person, and his name is Jesus! He comes to you and makes a commitment of hope: "And behold, I am with you always, to the end of the age" (Matthew 28:20).[2]

—Paul Tripp

TWENTY-SIX

WHO'S IN CONTROL WHEN LIFE HURTS?

We Don't Know *Why*, We Only Know *Who*

Is the gospel Seth believed in a sham?
Where was his God, the Bible's great "I AM"
when Seth tumbled off a Peruvian hill?
How was his tragic death a good Father's will?

Our finite minds cannot make any sense
of our God's dark, painful providence.
Why take one so young? Whose faith so true?
*We don't know **why**. We only know **Who**.*

Jesus moved into our neighborhood.
Fully God, fully man, He understood
that He was born to die, taking our place.
Our standing with God isn't earned—it's grace!
The cross: God's justice and love converged,
where our guilt and shame over sin was purged.
God knows our pain. He, too, suffered loss:

His nail-pierced Son upon Calvary's cross.

God isn't remote, or ever out of touch.
The cross shouts, "I love you this much!"
There Jesus accomplished "the death of death."
Seth knew this when he took his last breath.
Seth's life is not over. He's now complete.
He enjoys "Son-bathing" at His Savior's feet.
Losing him hurts, but the parting is brief.
For now, God's presence assuages our grief.

This life is short, but eternity is long.
The stakes are too high to get this wrong.
Yield to the cross for your heart's deepest needs.
Heed its call to serve, wherever that leads.
No wonder Seth loved the cross: that's where
he found a love that he wanted to share.
Though Seth now enjoys a different view,
*we do not know **why**, we only know **Who.***

————

A Tragic Death and Inevitable Questions

Seth Thomas, 24, died June 23, 2017 in a fall off a mountain in Peru.

He served on a mission team consisting of medical students and faculty from the University of South Carolina. In an impoverished area, they gave women exams to detect cervical cancer early, then, if necessary, performed surgery that could save their lives.

Seth attended my local church in South Carolina. Exceptionally gifted intellectually, Seth also exhibited a soft heart toward God and people in need.

He loved to pray and worship God from high geographical vantage points, such as mountain peaks. On Friday afternoon, June 23, wooed by a large cross on a small plateau at the top of a 14,000-foot peak, he took off by himself on a three-hour hike with food, a blanket, his Bible and a flashlight. He never returned. Searches found his body two days later.

After receiving his medical degree, this godly young man anticipated serving Christ by devoting part of every year to mission work. I wrestled with the inevitable "Why?" question. Why did one so young, with such potential for the Lord, die? Could I reconcile his death with a wise, good and loving God? Those questions prompted the poem, which I read at Seth's memorial service.

Since the birth of Christianity, scholars and apologists have dealt with the "Why?" question in relation to suffering. I can't satisfactorily explain it. But it's my rock-ribbed conviction that what we know about God, from the Bible as well as our personal pilgrimage, is more helpful than trying to figure out why such seemingly pointless tragedies occur. Perhaps it seems overly simplistic, but when we don't know *why*, we can know *who* is in control.

I'll focus on one truth about God that should affect how we respond to suffering: *God's sovereignty*, the conviction that He controls both human actions and natural events. It is a mysterious yet priceless truth. No, meditating on it won't rescue us from the hurt that comes with suffering, but over the long haul, resting in it may assuage our grief and offer a helpful perspective.

Vaneetha's Comfort

Vaneetha Risner is a Christ-follower who experienced severe suffering: the loss of a baby due to a physician's mistake, post-polio syndrome that began ravishing her body when in her 30s, and the abandonment of her husband, leaving her with two girls to raise on her own while her physical strength waned. In a post titled, "Is My Suffering Meaningless?," she explained how belief in God's sovereignty carried her through the afflictions:

> I met with a friend who believes that while God draws near to us in our trials, people often suffer in ways that God never intended. God reacts to our suffering but never causes it. To her, the view that God has ordained all our suffering is inhumane. She sees it as completely against God's loving character: hurtful at best, and vindictive at worst.
>
> Personally, I couldn't disagree more.
>
> The truth of God's sovereign control has offered me life-giving hope in the wake of unspeakable sorrow. I understand it sounds cruel to say that God willed my infant son's death. But believing that my son died against God's will is far worse. That would mean that God is not in control, evil can ultimately win, and my future is uncertain. Moreover, it would mean that my son's death was random. Meaningless. Without purpose.

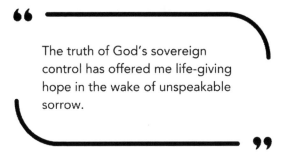

> The truth of God's sovereign control has offered me life-giving hope in the wake of unspeakable sorrow.

I honestly cannot imagine a more depressing scenario. As someone who has endured adversity, my greatest comfort is knowing that God is sovereign. He has ordained all of my trials, and therefore my suffering has purpose.

That one word—purpose—changes everything. It comforts me when pain envelops me and darkness is my closest friend. God does not delight in my suffering, but weeps with me as he did in John 11 after Lazarus died. But his tears are not all that he gives me. God gives me hope and assurance that my suffering is not in vain. Just as Jesus cried with Mary before he raised Lazarus (John 11:32-35), the Lord cries with me, knowing he will redeem my suffering.

It is comforting to know that everything God sends is the best possible thing for me. Nothing can derail his plan. No sin, no accident, no affliction. Satan does not have the last word on my suffering; God does. He has decreed it all and will use it all. As we see in the book of Job, God is not reacting to Satan's agenda. God alone is in control of all things.[1]

Charles Spurgeon, the 19th-century British pastor who suffered debilitating pain from gout as well as occasional episodes of depression, offered a similar perspective: "It would be a very sharp and trying experience to me to think that I have an affliction which God never sent me, that the bitter cup was never filled by His hand, that my trials were never measured out by Him, nor sent to me by His arrangement of their weight and quantity."[2]

When We Can't Understand Why

God often reveals how He redeems our severe afflictions. We realize over time that the pain created a desperate dependence on Him and enhanced our intimacy with Him. We see how the pain, even when our sin wasn't the cause, purified our character. We identify ways in which adversity expanded our capacity to minister to other hurting people.

But we don't always see how God redeems our pain. That's when reliance on God's character, as reflected in the poem lyrics, is most essential.

Joe Bayly was an author and Christian publishing executive who lost three children to death, one of whom was a godly teen who died from injuries sustained in a sledding accident. I attended a workshop he led on dealing with a loved one's death. During a question-and-answer time, a participant said to him, "It must have been meaningful to you when you finally realized why God took your children."

In response, Bayly bristled: "I don't know why God took my children! If I understood why, I wouldn't need any faith!" Bayly and his wife didn't grasp why the deaths occurred, yet they kept trusting and serving the God who did understand.

Resources

I highly recommend two books by Vaneetha Risner: *The Scars That Have Shaped Me: How God Meets Us in Suffering*[3] and *Walking Through Fire: A Memoir of Loss and Redemption*.[4] Joe Bayly wrote a helpful book on handling death and grief: *The View from a Hearse: A Christian View of Death*.[5] To explore the theme of God's sovereignty and suffering in detail, read *Suffering and the Sovereignty of God*[6], edited by John Piper and Justin Taylor.

? Probes to Ponder

What was your reaction to Vaneetha Risner's reasoning and to Joe Bayly's reply?

Has God's Spirit ever mollified *your* pain through meditation on God's sovereignty?

When you're hurting, what other insights about God, or promises He provided in His Word, comfort and sustain you?

When you suffer, how do divine attributes such as good, wise and loving affect your view of His sovereignty?

Have you thanked the Lord for specific attributes that comfort you?

What questions about the relationship between suffering and the sovereignty of God still roil around in your mind?

Prayer Response

Father, in this life, I'll never grasp why every instance of suffering happens. Yet even when pain shreds my heart and alters my life, instead of resentment toward You taking root in my heart, help me to throw myself into Your strong arms and experience the comfort of Your love, even when You never explain why. When I hurt, meet me as a person so that awareness of Your presence more than compensates for the lack of explanations. In the name of the One who was called "man of sorrows and acquainted with grief" (Isaiah 53:3), amen.

  ## A Pertinent Word

In him we have obtained an inheritance, having been predestined according to the purpose of him who works all things according to the counsel of his will.

Ephesians 1:11

An Apt Quote

We all face things that appear to make little sense and don't seem to serve any good purpose. Rest is never found in the quest to understand it all. No, rest is found in trusting the One who understands it all and rules it all for his glory and our good. [7]

—Paul Tripp

TWENTY-SEVEN
HOW DO YOU GO HIGHER WITH GOD?

At Jesus' Feet

At the feet of Jesus, I thank Him for His grace;
so rich and free, outpoured for me, that's where I put my face.

At the feet of Jesus, I lay my deepest needs.
The load is there for Him to bear; He hears the heart that pleads.

At the feet of Jesus, I confess all my sins.
His sacrifice paid their full price; my brokenness He mends.

At the feet of Jesus, when my weak hands are tied,
I make a plea for family to walk close by His side.

At the feet of Jesus, I get a better view
of who He is, the might that's His. I give the praise He's due.

At the feet of Jesus, I listen to Him talk.
What I have heard within His Word sustains my daily walk.

At the feet of Jesus, demons bow in one accord:
they cower before His power, acknowledging Him as Lord.

———

The Way Up with God Is Down

The most soul-nourishing topical study I've ever undertaken took me to all the New Testament verses that mention the feet of Jesus, or which show someone bowing before Him. What I learned inspired this poem.

Most references occur in the four Gospels, where people literally fell at His feet for a variety of compelling reasons. Christ-followers today can't bow before His physical body—that occurs later when we meet Him face to face! Yet meditating on the narratives where individuals wound up at His feet offers rich insights, demonstrating the posture of mind and heart that Christ desires when we approach Him in prayer.

Each short stanza in the poem captures a specific reason that someone who encountered Jesus fell or bowed at Jesus' feet. We may approach Him for the same burdens and needs.

When and How to Approach the Lord

Here are the primary texts that I examined. Each set of texts covers one main reason someone (or a group) fell at His feet, or in one case will do so in the future.

1. Luke 10:38-42
2. Matthew 15:21-31; Luke 8:41-48
3. Luke 8:26-39 (especially verse 35), 17:11-19

4. Luke 5:1-8, 7:36-50
5. Matthew 17:1-8; Mark 3:11, 5:1-7; Philippians 2:9-11; Revelation 1:9-18
6. Matthew 28:1-9; Revelation 4:8-11, 5 (entire chapter, especially verses 8 and 14), 7:9-12

When you have time, examine each passage slowly and consider the following questions.

- Who fell at Jesus' feet?
- Why did each person approach Him?
- How did Jesus respond to the person?
- What words best describe the mindset or attitude of the people who approached Him?

In most verses you consult, you'll find answers to all the questions. In a few instances, the text says someone bowed or fell before Him, but most of the time there's a literal reference to Jesus' feet.

For me, the ultimate outcome was a keener sensitivity to the Holy Spirit, to the times when He is nudging me to fall at the Savior's feet for one reason or another.

What follows is a basic summary of my findings, categorizing the various reasons people fell at His feet.

1. **To Receive Instruction** Luke 10:38-42
2. **To Request Help** Matthew 15:21-31; Luke 8:41-48
3. **To Reveal Gratitude** Luke 8:26-39 (especially verse 35), 17:11-19
4. **To Renounce Sin** Luke 5:1-8, 7: 36-50

5. **To Recognize His Authority** Matthew 17:1-8; Mark 3:11, 5:1-7; Philippians 2:9-11; Revelation 1:9-18.

6. **To Revel in His Presence (Worship and Praise)** Matthew 28:1-9; Revelation 4:8-11, 5 (entire chapter, especially verses 8 and 14), 7:9-12

You'll discover that the proper etiquette for approaching our Lord is face down, propelled by a spirit of desperation, humility or awe. You'll be far less likely to approach Him glibly.

No matter how many people fall at Jesus' feet, there's always room for one more.

Will that one be you?

? Probes to Ponder

You saw that individuals and groups fell at Jesus' feet for various reasons. Why do you need to fall at His feet today?

Which incident I cited from the New Testament encourages you most today? Why?

What do you learn about Jesus from those narratives?

What attitude or "posture of the heart" did those who fell at Jesus' feet demonstrate?

How should the references to Jesus' feet (or bowing before Him) affect your prayer life?

Prayer Response

O Lord, keep reminding me that when I feel most desperate and lowly, You are most gracious toward me. When I fall at Your feet, whether physically prostrate or if that's merely the posture of my heart while lying in bed, You are pleased. Never let me forget that having nowhere to look but up is a strategic vantage point! In the name of the One before whom every knee will eventually bow (Philippians 2:9-11), amen.

 A Pertinent Word

Clothe yourselves, all of you, with humility toward one another, for 'God opposes the proud but gives grace to the humble.' Humble yourselves, therefore, under the mighty hand of God so that at the proper time he may exalt you.

1 Peter 5:5-6

 An Apt Quote

Here is the path to the higher life: down, lower down! Just as water always seeks and fills the lowest place, so the moment God finds men abased and empty, His glory and power flow in to exalt and to bless.[1]

—Andrew Murray, *Humility: The Journey Toward Holiness*

TWENTY-EIGHT
ARE YOU DISCOURAGED ABOUT YOUR WEAKNESSES?

My Source of Strength

*When I'm in the dark I look at the Light
who can turn my night into day;
who creates in me new eyes that can see
the good He has sent my way.*

*When I feel down, then I look up
to the One who is my hope.
When I'm afraid I seek the aid
of the One who helps me cope.*

*When I feel faint I rest on the Rock;
He's secure, steady and strong.
When I feel heat I fall at the feet
of One who can right what's wrong.*

*When I am all spent and I need to vent,
He's the One whose ear I seek.*

When I'm flat on my face, He gives His grace;
He is stronger than I am weak.

———

What inspired these lyrics? Frustration concerning areas of personal weakness and inadequacy, countered by meditation on God's Word, which offered a reassuring perspective.

Discouraged Over Deficiencies

What weaknesses in yourself do you deplore? In what area do you see yourself as most vulnerable to temptation? What mistakes or poor decisions still haunt you? In relation to your temperament or personality, do you ever wish that God had put you together differently?

For most of my life, I've bucked against certain frailties and limitations. I often view my weaknesses as things that must be overcome, feeling frustrated when, decade after decade of my spiritual pilgrimage, I still exhibit those deficiencies or imperfections.

I've lamented a hypersensitivity that leaves me easily hurt by people or life events. I'm so needy and insecure in my relationships, I wonder why God created me with such thin skin.

I've bemoaned my genetic predisposition to depression because it's downright draining to fight pessimistic thoughts and harmful emotions.

I get discouraged because I'm still extremely vulnerable to temptation. I'm aware that temptation itself isn't sin, yet I criticize myself because I think I yield far too often for a man who has been a believer for six decades. I figure that I'm in pre-kindergarten, spiritually speaking. I know I must not tolerate sin, yet in the process of my ups and downs in following Christ, I've never exercised much grace or patience in relation to myself.

More recently, I've brooded over my physical decline, which includes escalating pain and energy depletion. I realize that no one who lives past middle age escapes the signs of aging. I just don't like living in an increasing state of neediness.

In a nutshell, I don't like feeling out of control or weak. I've often said to myself, "What's the matter with you!?"

Duh—I'm human!

And I'm discovering why that's okay. Now I strive to see Jesus' cross clearly, rather than turn my focus inward. His sufficiency, not my deficiencies, must become my obsession.

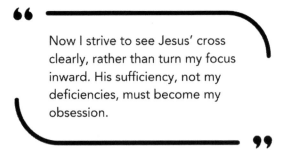

> Now I strive to see Jesus' cross clearly, rather than turn my focus inward. His sufficiency, not my deficiencies, must become my obsession.

God's Perspective on Our Weaknesses

Thankfully, I'm becoming more alert to the numerous biblical references that describe us as desperate, needy creatures. God goes to great pains within His Word to say that we're prone to anxiety and fears. The Bible assumes that we can't always manage our lives well. His Word acknowledges the inevitability of weariness, temptations, burdens, bodily decline and various trials that tax our reserves.

Bible verses such as the ones that follow are ever-so-slowly allowing me to accept my finiteness and view my weaknesses as an opportunity to experience God's grace. I'm beginning to chafe less about my deficiencies, to accept the fact that I'm needy and always will be.

- "Why are you cast down, O my soul, and why are you in turmoil within me? Hope in God; for I shall again praise him, my salvation and my God" (Psalm 42:11).
- "Cast your burden on the Lord and he will sustain you" (Psalm 55:22).
- "On God rests my salvation and my glory; my mighty rock, my refuge is God. Trust in him at all times, O people; pour out your heart before him; God is a refuge for us" (Psalm 62:7-8).
- "My flesh and my heart may fail, but God is the strength of my heart and my portion forever" (Psalm 73:26).
- "Trust in the Lord with all your heart, and do not lean on your own understanding. In all your ways acknowledge him and he will make your paths straight. Be not wise in your own eyes" (Proverbs 3:5-7a).
- "Fear not, for I am with you; be not dismayed, for I am your God; I will strengthen you, I will help you,

I will uphold you with my righteous right hand"
(Isaiah 41:10).

- "Rejoice not over me, O my enemy; when I fall, I
  shall rise; when I sit in darkness, the Lord will be a
  light to me" (Micah 7:8).
- "Come to Me, all who labor and are heavy laden,
  and I will give you rest" (Matthew 11:28).
- In reference to our resurrected body, Paul wrote,
  "What is sown is perishable; what is raised is
  imperishable. It is sown in dishonor; it is raised in
  glory. It is sown in weakness; it is raised in power" (1
  Corinthians 15:42-43).

Why Weakness Is Okay

In *New Morning Mercies,* a 365-day devotional book, Paul
Tripp elaborates on the importance of admitting our
neediness:

> We don't like facing the truth that we're all weak in our own
> ways. It is the universal condition of humanity...Weakness is
> not the big danger to be avoided. What you need to avoid is
> your delusion of strength.

> We are weak in wisdom, weak in strength, weak in right-
> eousness. Sin has left us weak of heart and hands. It has left
> us feeble and lame in many ways. But God's grace makes
> weakness a thing to be feared no longer. The God of grace
> who calls you to himself and calls you to live for him blesses
> you with all the strength you need to do what he's called
> you to do. The way to enter into that strength is to admit
> how little strength you actually have. Grace frees me from

being devastated that I can no longer trust me because grace connects me to One who is worthy of my trust and who will always deliver what I need.

We're created to be dependent on God. We all need strength beyond our own and power that we'll never independently possess. So God, in grace, grants us power in the person of the Holy Spirit, who lives inside each of his children. [1]

If you were totally adequate for running your life, you wouldn't need God. To use the analogy of Paul's thorn in the flesh, which he thought limited his life and ministry, stop trying to yank out your thorns (2 Corinthians 12:7-10).

Your frailties and limitations create a desperate dependence on God, and that's a good thing. I've often said this to my students: *It's okay if you see me as weak and inadequate, as long as you see that the Christ on whom I lean is strong and capable!*

? Probes to Ponder

Reserve a devotional time to read the verses again from the "God's Perspective on Our Weaknesses" section. Then prayerfully mull over these questions.

Which Bible verse resonates most with you today? Why? Memorize it so the Holy Spirit will bring His Word to your mind when you need it.

From this compilation of verses, what words and phrases reveal something encouraging about the nature of God?

What words and phrases offer a promise of what God will do for and in you?

What do these verses instruct you to do in response to your limitations? (Pick out words that call for action on your part.)

Based on the cumulative input from these texts, how would you complete this sentence? "It's okay to be weak and needy because _____."

 Prayer Response

Father, You want me to work on some areas of weakness. When a pattern of sin is involved, I must pursue holiness aggressively (Hebrews 12:14). Yet other areas of weakness or inadequacy I must accept. Please give me the discernment to know the difference, so I don't strive for perfectionism in an unhealthy manner, so I'll treat myself as graciously as You treat me. Help me to see, day in and day out, that my weaknesses provide more reason to lean on You. In the name of Your Son, the only man in history who had it all together, amen.

A Pertinent Word

But we have this treasure in jars of clay, to show that the surpassing power belongs to God and not to us.

2 Corinthians 4:7

"" An Apt Quote

Grace is God drawing us sinners closer and closer to Himself. And how does God in grace prosecute this purpose? Not by shielding us from assault by the world, the flesh and the devil, nor by protecting us from burdensome and frustrating circumstances, nor by shielding us from troubles created by our own temperament and psychology; but rather by exposing us to all these things, so as to overwhelm us with a sense of our own inadequacy, and to drive us to cling to Him more closely. This is the ultimate reason why God fills our lives with troubles and perplexities of one sort or another. It is to ensure that we shall learn to hold Him fast. He takes steps to drive us out of self-confidence to trust in Himself.[2]

—J.I. Packer, *Knowing God*

TWENTY-NINE

DO YOU KNOW ANY HOMELESS PEOPLE?

Homeless

Their estate? In the bag they tote.
Blotches of dirt caked on their coat.
Eyelids droop. It's night that they dread:
a bench or grass becomes their bed.

Their stomach growls. What will they eat?
They scrounge for change along the street,
or search for scraps tossed in the trash
when cost of food exceeds their cash.

A heavy heart shows on their face.
No hand to hold. No firm embrace.
No laughter heard in a warm den
when spouse or children saunter in.

What pain: to live each day alone.
No family to call their own.

There's little hope for a fresh start.
No one to fill their empty heart.

Some folks are blessed with worldly worth,
yet have not had a second birth.
They lie in comfort, yet some weep;
their heavy hearts cannot find sleep.
No matter how they dress, their heart
is still tattooed with Satan's art,
not scrubbed clean by Jesus' blood.
No Spirit there to stem sin's flood.

Stomachs full of meat and bread.
It's their soul that's underfed.
They live, without knowing why.
No plan to live after they die.
No purpose in the day's routine.
No Timeless Truth on which to lean.

They experiment with zeal
for ways a Christ-shaped void to fill.
They do not bear the Savior's name;
no divine inheritance to claim.
No larger group of blood-bought kin
to stand with them through thick and thin.

When they are feeling incomplete;
when living hurts or brings defeat,
there's no respite at Jesus' feet.
Poorer than those who roam the street.

The poem mentions two types of homelessness: the poor who go without a physical residence, and persons without Christ, who don't look forward to an eternal home in heaven.

Hungry and Without Shelter

In cities across the United States, homeless individuals sleep on park benches, under bridges and on scraps of cardboard stretched out on sidewalks. In the suburbs of my hometown of Columbia, South Carolina, on busy street corners where there's a traffic light, they hold up tattered, hand-lettered signs telling you they're hungry and need cash for food.

Homelessness is more rampant in countries such as India, where millions either live in slums, under bridges or on the streets. I've observed acre after acre of shanties in a slum adjacent to the Mumbai airport, where large families live in a one-room, bathroom-sized dirt floor "house" with no running water or electricity, their shelter often no more than tin, cardboard or dirty cloths.

Outside the small motel in Mumbai where my wife and I stayed for a few hours between flights, folks slept on the sidewalk, their cardboard "walls" shaped like teepees to keep out intruders and the chill. When we took a taxi to the airport after midnight, scores of people, including kids, hunkered down under a bridge we crossed.

After my third teaching trip to India, I realized how financially wealthy I am. What I had perceived as the meager salary of a Bible college professor is relative. My salary put me in the top one percent of wealth in the world!

God's Heart for the Poor

The Bible teems with God's concern for the needy and His desire that His people involve themselves with the poor. Proverbs 19:17 represents multiple verses in the book that reveal His heart: "Whoever is generous to the poor lends to the Lord, and he will repay him for his deed." The God who made heaven and earth is the One "who executes justice for the oppressed, who gives food to the hungry" (Psalm 146:7).

According to Luke 12:33, God expects His people to share His burden for those who suffer, and that includes generosity to the needy. In James 1:27, pure and undefiled religion includes visiting "orphans and widows in their affliction." In Matthew 25:31-40, Jesus put an exclamation point on serving those with material needs. He envisioned His throne in heaven, when the righteous would ask Him this question: "Lord, when did we see you hungry and feed you, or thirsty and give you drink? And when did we see you a stranger and welcome you, or naked and clothe you? And when did we see you sick or in prison and visit you?"

His reply? "Truly, I say to you, as you did it to one of the least of these my brothers, you did it to me."

Many denominations and local churches operate a "Justice and Mercy" ministry to meet pressing physical and material needs of people. Reputable organizations exist to solicit resources from God's people to serve the poor overseas.

Perhaps your community includes a gospel-centered mission or agencies that exist to serve those in need.

Yet the other form of homelessness mentioned in the last few stanzas of the poem is an even higher priority: *those without the assurance of a forever home in heaven.* Christ wants us to minister to the physical needs of the poor in responsible ways, yet spiritual poverty is more tragic because it metes out eternal consequences.

> **"**
> Christ wants us to minister to the physical needs of the poor in responsible ways, yet spiritual poverty is more tragic because it metes out eternal consequences.
> **"**

A Forever Home

Anyone biblically literate sees God's concern for those who haven't put faith in Christ. The theme of spreading the gospel —communicating the good news of Jesus' sacrifice on the cross for sin—stitches together the pages of the New Testament.

Concerning the content of the gospel, God the Father's love for mankind prompted Him to send His Son to earth (John 3:16-17). Jesus' death on the cross paid the penalty for sin for whoever trusts in Him (2 Corinthians 5:21). As a result, a Christian is reconciled to a holy God, because Christ's righteousness was imputed to him (Romans 5:6-10). Christ's resurrection from the dead confirmed His divinity (1 Corinthians 15:1-8). The Bible clearly teaches the exclusiveness of Christianity: faith in Jesus is the only way to enter a relationship with God (John 14:6; Acts 4:12).

Christ-followers possess the call and privilege to share this good news! Jesus lamented that the harvest is plentiful, but laborers are few. That's why He told us to "pray earnestly to the Lord of the harvest to send out laborers" (Matthew 9:38). His final commission to the church was to "make disciples of all nations" (Matthew 28:19), which begins with evangelism and includes ongoing nurture of believers.

According to Paul, before anyone believes the gospel, someone must share the good news of Christ (Romans 10:9-15). Though not every Christian participates in God's plan of redemption in the same way, each of us is an ambassador—an official representative of Christ on earth. In some form, each of us has been given a "ministry of reconciliation" (2 Corinthians 5:15-21).

Unconditional Love

Yet communicating the gospel isn't merely a matter of comprehending its message, of cognitively mastering steps (truths) in the plan of salvation. It isn't a matter of fulfilling a duty, something we *ought* to do as a Christ-follower. No, it's about being so overwhelmed by the love we've received from the Lord that we want to share it. It's about a God who "shows his love for us in that while we were still sinners, Christ died for us" (Romans 5:8).

It's personal to God.

It's about iron spikes shredding the skin of our Savior; about His blood splattered all over those wooden beams. It's about a Savior whose arms were stretched out to either side as far as they could go, and, in effect, crying out, *"This much I love you!"* Despite the horrendous pain, the gospel features a Savior "who for the joy set before him endured the cross" (Hebrews 12:2).

It's personal to God, who forsook His Son on the cross so He wouldn't forsake us.

Evangelism is a cross in the heart of God. How well do you see the cross on which Jesus died?

?   Probes to Ponder

Within your family, or among your neighbors and work associates, for whom are you spiritually burdened? Plea for God's Spirit to open the filters of their mind to the gospel, to soften their heart so there's more receptivity when you talk about the Savior.

Though God employs human instruments to share the gospel, conversion is a supernatural work of His Spirit. In Acts 16:14, concerning Lydia's conversion, notice the wording: *"The Lord opened her heart* to pay attention to what Paul said" (emphasis mine). Our application of this truth is to intercede for lost persons and efforts to reach them.

What will you do to build closer relationships with unbelievers? Though your love for and attention to them shouldn't hinge on whether they put faith in Christ, nonetheless your efforts at building a relationship may provide greater opportunities to share the gospel with them.

What agencies and organizations in your area serve the poor and homeless? Do these ministries need funds or volunteers? How will your family, small group or local church assist?

Will you minister to both types of homeless persons? John Mott aptly said, "Evangelism, without social action, is deficient; social work without evangelism is impotent."[1]

 Prayer Response

Oh God, prompt me to serve the physical needs of others regardless of whether they put their faith in Christ. And help me to offer a winsome verbal explanation of the gospel to those who don't know You, whether they're rich or poor materially. In the name of Jesus, who was rich, then became poor, that out of our spiritual poverty we might become rich in spiritual blessings, amen.

 A Pertinent Word

All this is from God, who through Christ reconciled us to himself and gave us the ministry of reconciliation; that is, in Christ God was reconciling the world to himself, not counting their trespasses against them, and entrusting to us the message of reconciliation. Therefore, we are ambassadors for Christ, God making his appeal through us. We implore you on behalf of Christ, be reconciled to God.

2 Corinthians 5:18-20

❝❞ An Apt Quote

Social action is a partner of evangelism. As partners, the two belong to each other and yet are independent of each other. Both are expressions of unfeigned love, to see need and possess the remedy compels us to act.

We are sent into the world, like Jesus, to serve. And in this we should have no ulterior motive. True, the gospel lacks visibility if we merely preach it, and lacks credibility if we who preach it are only interested in souls and have no concern about the welfare of people's bodies, situations, and communities. Yet the reason for our acceptance of social responsibility is not primarily to the give the gospel visibility or credibility it would otherwise lack but simple, uncomplicated compassion. Love has no need to justify itself. It merely expresses itself in service wherever it sees need.[2]

—John Stott

THIRTY

HOW WILL GOD USE YOU TO ENCOURAGE OTHERS?

God's Best

Both joy and hurt vie for a place
within your heart today.
Both smiles and tears form on your face
when Andrew is on display.
You lean upon the Lord's rich grace,
and make His strength your stay.

I cannot say "I understand."
I do not know your pain.
I can't convey how God has planned
this grim circumstance for gain.
Right now, you may not see His hand;
to look for it could be in vain.

Yet I will pledge to intercede
for inward peace and rest;
for you to view him as a seed

who'll sprout into God's best;
for God to meet your every need
and show how you are blessed.

———

A Blessing Named Andrew

The wife of a faculty colleague at Columbia International University gave birth to a boy with Down's Syndrome. He arrived about 17 years after the birth of their daughter. They didn't know in advance that Andrew would leave the womb with Down's Syndrome. I wanted them to know I was thinking of them and praying for them.

Prior to Andrew's birth, I had heard from several couples who parented Down's Syndrome children. Each couple conveyed that over the years, their son or daughter developed into an extremely warm, loving person. They testified that their infant became a blessing, not an inconvenience, who instilled delight and gratitude within them. That's a perspective I wanted to capture in the poem I wrote for them.

Serving Those Who Suffer

I'm melancholy, prone to self-absorption. Knowing that, a long time ago I asked the Lord to increase my sensitivity to others who suffer, to show me how I can best serve them. He occasionally nudges me to write the hurting person a poem. It's the most personal gift I can possibly give someone since the words stem from my heart, not just from my mind.

Perhaps you aren't a poet, but God has put you together in some manner that enables you to exercise a ministry of encouragement. If He can use an introverted person like me in that capacity, He can and will employ you to massage the hearts of others. Besides, encouraging others is a command for Christ-followers. After citing the benefit of eternal life through faith in Christ, Paul told his readers to "Encourage one another and build one another up, just as you are doing" (1 Thessalonians 5:11).

> **"**
>
> God has put you together in some manner that enables you to exercise a ministry of encouragement.
>
> **"**

Update on Andrew

I asked Andrew's dad, David Olshine, to give an update on the blessing Andrew has been to him and to his wife, Rhonda.

Within hours of Andrew's birth in 2002, a specialist informed us of his Down's Syndrome. For a month, fears and worries surfaced. I wondered, "Will Andrew live a long life? What will it be like to have a child with a disability?" I remember thinking, "I can't imagine living with a child like this!" I even prayed that God would "un-down" Andrew's Down's Syndrome:

In retrospect, Rhonda and I thank God for Andrew! He loves everyone he meets. He makes everyone's day brighter. He's witty, insightful and intelligent (reading at a 10th-grade level). He doesn't let his limitations keep him from experiencing a full life. Andrew swam on his high school swim team. He worked to become proficient in paddle boarding, ping pong, tennis and computer usage. He enjoys travel and experiencing new adventures.

What has Andrew done for me personally? God used him to change me. I'm a more sensitive person now, less judgmental toward people. I'm more sensitive toward others when they encounter trials. I'm especially more compassionate toward persons with special needs who I see in public, offering to lend them a hand when it's needed.

Twenty years ago, I thought, "I can't imagine living with a child like this!" Now I think, "I can't imagine living my life without Andrew!"

(In 2022, David released a book that includes, but isn't limited to, Andrew's story. You'll profit immensely by reading *The Mystery of Silence: Making Sense of Life When God Seems Absent.*[1])

? Probes to Ponder

In your sphere of influence, who currently needs some form of encouragement? Does a member of your church, your pastor, a missionary or a neighbor come to mind? If not, ask the Lord to give you the name of someone who needs you to lift his or her spirit.

How has God uniquely created you and prepared you to serve others? He has given you talents, experiences and empathy that qualify you to reach out in an original way. Allow the following probes to serve as a catalyst for your thinking about the forms your future ministry of encouragement will take.

- When someone is needy or suffering, will you give the gift of your physical presence, even when you're unsure of what to say? Will you allow your nearness to express what mere words cannot?
- Does your baking elicit moans of mouth-watering pleasure when your cakes, cookies or brownies mingle with others' taste buds? Will dropping off a treat or a food gift to someone who's sick or hurting bring delight to their heart—and to yours?
- Perhaps you've read a grace-saturated book that strengthened you. Will you send a new copy, with a personal note, to someone who's suffering or grieving a loss?
- Will you write a reassuring note in which you share a Bible verse or truth, and explain how it rejuvenated you, in a way that won't be perceived as preachy or superficial?
- Will you exercise a ministry of help by performing a necessary chore for someone who isn't able to do it, such as mowing the lawn or cooking a meal?

 Prayer Response

Father, numerous times You've embodied Your love to me through another Christian who came alongside me. Please enable me to

give others a jumpstart when their emotional battery is low. In the name of Your Son, who offered the supreme example of presence when He "became flesh and dwelt among us" (John 1:14), amen.

 ## A Pertinent Word

Let us consider how to stir up one another to love and good works, not neglecting to meet together, as is the habit of some, but encouraging one another, all the more as you see the Day drawing near.

Hebrews 10:24-25

 ## An Apt Quote

Everyone has the potential to become an encourager. You don't have to be rich. You don't have to be a genius. You don't have to have it all together. All you have to do is care about people and take initiative. [2]

—John Maxwell

THIRTY-ONE
DO YOU WANT TO LIVE BEFORE YOU DIE?

I Want to *Live* Before I Die!

I want to live before I die;
to laugh aloud more than I cry.
To wake each day with gratitude;
to don a cheerful attitude.
To trust Christ more and worry less.
To live, less sensitive to stress.
When trials come, stay undeterred,
fueled by the truths within God's Word.
To know that pain is temporary.
When I'm needy, grace won't tarry,
for God is good and in control;
my joy and fruitfulness, His goal.
To believe He'll redeem my pain.
Since He is wise, then why complain?
I want to live before I die!
To smile more often than I sigh,
my merry countenance revealing

that life with Jesus is appealing.

To take my bride on day-long dates
before my health deteriorates.
To fly a kite with my grandson.
Ride waterslides—oh my, what fun!
Take each grown son on a long trip;
become a friend, build fellowship.

To pause and watch as squirrels play.
To smell gardenias in May.
To search for rainbows in the sky.
Watch sparrows frolic while they fly.
To squish dewdrops with my bare feet
before they're gone, dispelled by heat.
To watch a cat licking his paw,
then wash his face and head. What awe!

To serve God, yes, but not ignore
my need for rest. Less becomes more!
My schedule needs an overhaul.
Not every need is the Lord's call.
I'll recall times I've imploded
so I won't get overloaded.
Say "No" often. The reason why?
My God will live after I die!

Then when it's time for me to die
I'll bid all pain and tears goodbye.
No more despondency or loss;
I'll Sonbathe in rays from the cross.
I'll see my Savior face to face;

exult in His breathtaking grace.

A Time for Change

As a new year approaches, or shortly after it begins, do you reflect on areas in which you see a need to change? Do you ask God to reveal areas of life in which He desires renewal for you?

Do you view January 1 as an opportune time to evaluate personal priorities, to identify necessary changes in your expenditure of time and energy?

Is the Spirit of God at work within you, causing turbulence or discontent concerning areas that He wants to overhaul?

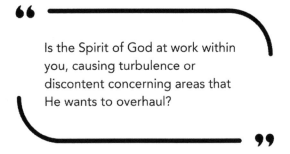

> Is the Spirit of God at work within you, causing turbulence or discontent concerning areas that He wants to overhaul?

As 2022 began, my response to those questions was an unequivocal "Yes!" I chose a single word, prayerfully considered, that captured how I wanted God to work in my life during the new year: *change.*

I didn't write specific resolutions for key areas of my life. Rather, my reflections resulted in the poem, "I Want to *Live* Before I Die."

The lyrics refer to areas of life where I felt a strong nudge of God's Spirit to change: my reactions to physical pain and decline; my tendency to focus on depression symptoms rather than reasons for joy; a need to spend more time with immediate family members, and to choose more rest and play to complement ongoing ministry opportunities during retirement.

Yes, your needs differ. Yet I believe the process the Holy Spirit took me through will spur your own thinking about necessary adjustments that He wants *you* to make. Be teachable concerning what the Holy Spirit whispers to you as I explain thought processes He took me through prior to writing the poem.

What Inspired the Poem?

Implications of Belief

The first stanza, prior to the first line of white space, reveals my desire to balance the gloominess that typically accompanies depression episodes with more positive attitudes, such as gratitude. To believe that God is good and sovereign, even over the recent escalation of bodily pain and my continued vulnerability to dips in spirit.

Does my downcast countenance indicate that I don't *really* believe God is sovereign? Without minimizing the debilitating emotional pain that accompanies a depressive episode, can the primary trajectory of my life showcase the joy that God desires for His people?

Have I given excessive attention to the difficulty of living with a mental illness at the exclusion of reveling in the benefits of my faith in Christ? How do I reconcile a consistently downcast spirit with Jesus' teaching on the benefits of abiding in Him, as seen in John 15:11? "These things I have spoken to you, that my joy may be in you, and that your joy may be full."

Family Relationships

The second stanza reveals my felt need, implanted by the Lord, for giving more time to my family relationships. Such changes necessarily involve *time*. During a recent prayer time, the Holy Spirit reminded me of a gravestone epitaph. Someone chiseled these words along the top: *Here lies a man who was always going to....* Then, across the bottom of the gravestone, you see these words: *Now he's gone.*

Noticing Nature

The third stanza reveals my desire to notice the delights of nature and God's creation, including the animal kingdom. The prolific 19th-century preacher, Charles Spurgeon, often found relief from discouragement by taking long walks and observing the natural beauty of the outdoors. Spurgeon's focus on nature ramped up his happiness and evoked praise within him for God and His attribute of creativity. I want to exult in God through appreciation of His creation, as David did. "O

Lord, our Lord, how majestic is your name in all the earth! You have set your glory above the heavens" (Psalm 8:1).

Selectivity in Choosing Ministries

In the fourth stanza, I acknowledge that my ministry calling didn't end when I retired from full-time teaching. On the other hand, due to declining energy and physical infirmities that accompany aging, I must choose wisely and not view every opportunity offered to me as God's will for my life. If I'm more discriminating in choosing what to write and how often to teach or to preach, I'll reserve the physical, mental and emotional margin that's necessary for implementing the needed areas of change cited in the previous stanzas.

Ironically, *doing less for the Lord may enable me to accomplish more for Him.*

As I wrote the last two lines of the fourth stanza, I remembered this maxim: *Cemeteries are filled with indispensable people.* Also, throughout this reassessment process, a remark from missionary martyr Jim Elliot kept goading me: "When it comes time for you to die, see to it that all you have left to do is die."[1]

Why Dying Is Gain

The final stanza cites the wonderful anticipation of seeing the Savior face to face in the new heaven and new earth, where God "will wipe away every tear from their eyes, and death shall be no more, neither shall there be mourning, nor crying, nor pain anymore" (Revelation 21:4).

? Probes to Ponder

I want to live before I die. Do you?

Cup your ears. Do you hear Him? Listen carefully. What is God's Spirit whispering to you right now concerning personal priorities and areas He wants to transform?

How can you cooperate with the Lord in the spheres of your life that need renewal? In what ways can you tap into His power to effect changes that require more than mere fleshly effort?

Identify a brother or sister in the Lord whom you respect. Share with this individual your answers to the previous questions. Invite him or her to hold you accountable for the actions you must take so your resolve takes concrete form.

Prayer Response

Father, empower me to live in a way that will result in fewer regrets and in a manner that will reflect Your values and priorities. Help me to accomplish all You want me to do in this life—no more and no less. In the name of Jesus, who confidently proclaimed this in a prayer to You: "I glorified you on earth, having accomplished the work which you gave me to do" (John 17:4). So very amen!

A Pertinent Word

The thief comes only to steal and kill and destroy. I came that they may have life and have it abundantly.

John 10:10

 An Apt Quote

We change our behavior when the pain of staying the same becomes greater than the pain of changing.[2]

—Peter Scazzero

ABOUT THE AUTHOR

Terry Powell is Faculty Emeritus in Church Ministry at Columbia International University in South Carolina, where he taught for 38 years. He served as a Christian Education Director on two  church staffs for a total of 12 years and he's a licensed preacher in the PCA (Presbyterian Church in America). Terry has taught and trained national Christian leaders overseas in numerous countries.

He's the author of 20 books and writes a blog on depression and faith at penetratingthedarkness.com. In addition to his bride of over 52 years, Terry has two grown sons, a daughter-in-law and a grandson. His hobbies include reading novels and writing poetry. His constant prayer is, "Lord, make me half the man my dog thinks I am!"

To contact the author, email him at terry.powell@ciu.edu

ENCOURAGEMENT FOR PASTORS, MISSIONARIES AND BIBLE STUDY LEADERS

Serve Strong: Biblical Encouragement to Sustain God's Servants by Terry Powell (Leafwood Books)

Are you weary from overwork, feeling inadequate, doubting God's call on your life, seeing no fruit or fatigued by spiritual warfare? Is your passion and motivation for ministry waning?

Or are you motivated and serving strong now, but interested in biblical truths that will continue to instill resiliency in the future?

Terry explains and illustrates Bible truths that have sustained him for over 50 years of full-time ministry. He also explains how God sustained historical figures like John Newton, David Brainerd, William Wilberforce, Charles Spurgeon, D.L. Moody, Saint Augustine and Hudson Taylor.

Learn how God uses pain, delays, brokenness and failure to expand your usefulness. Discover reasons why you shouldn't lose heart in your ministry, how God's definition of success in ministry differs from yours and how confidence in your service is not dependent on your own ability or experience.

Get a copy for yourself and a church staff member or missionary you want to encourage. Available at Amazon and other booksellers.

DO YOU WANT TO LEAD EVEN MORE EFFECTIVE GROUP BIBLE STUDIES?

NOW THAT'S A GOOD QUESTION! How To Lead Quality Bible Discussions by Terry Powell

A practical resource for small group leaders and classroom teachers of youth/adults. Terry addresses these questions, and much more!

- How can you create a hospitable group climate that expedites lively discussions?
- What are ways to apply the steps of inductive Bible study to *yourself* before you teach?
- How can you formulate better-worded questions that meet biblical and educational guidelines for excellence?
- How can you get more of your group members to participate?

- How can you prevent problems such as monopolizers, tangents, and a pooling of ignorance?
- How can you keep your group focused on what the Bible says and means so discussion doesn't degenerate into relativism?
- What are some get-acquainted or team-building ideas you can use in your group?

Find out why Andrew Mason, Senior Pastor and founder of smallgroupchurches.com, says, *"This book arms you with a weapons cache of knowledge, common mistakes to avoid and an arsenal of proven ideas and templates. It is a small group masterpiece."* Available at Amazon.

GOD SPEAKS THROUGH PAIN AND HE DOES NOT STUTTER!

Oh God, I'm Dying! How God Redeems Pain for Our Good and for His Glory by Terry Powell & Mark Smith

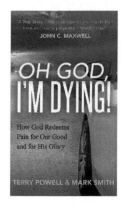

Oh God, I'm Dying is the riveting true story of Dr. Mark Smith, a high-profile Christian leader who has served effectively despite living with severe pain ever since a 1996 auto accident. He's the former president of Columbia International University in South Carolina. This book vividly describes the accident, the uncertainty and despondency he experienced during rehab, and illustrates the long-term physical consequences of a wreck caused by another person's carelessness.

The narrative *shows* Mark's experiences, rather than merely *describing* them. You'll see Mark's and his wife's desperate reliance on means of God's grace, including, but not limited to, heartfelt prayer, God's Word, others in the body of Christ,

Christian songs, and medical intervention. This book reveals how Mark's faith in Christ was tested, and ultimately deepened, due to the accident. Anyone who experiences physical pain or another form of ongoing affliction will discover the encouraging irony of how God redeems pain when He chooses not to remove it. The result of reading this story will be renewed hope that God can use broken people, enhancing their usefulness to Him not *in spite of suffering*, but *because* of it.

Available at Amazon and other booksellers.

NOTES

WHY READ THIS BOOK?

1. From Henri Nouwen, *Wounded Healer: Ministry in Contemporary Society*, Doubleday Image Book, 1979.

INTRODUCTION

1. Paul Tripp in a podcast titled, "Preach the Gospel to Yourself." In "The-ology Refresh: A Podcast for Christian Leaders," April 5, 2014.

1. CAN YOU SEE THE CROSS CLEARLY?

1. Robert McGee, *The Search for Significance: Seeing Your True Worth through God's Eyes* (Nashville: Thomas Nelson, 2003).
2. Melissa Kruger, Ed., *Identity Theft: Reclaiming the Truth of Who We Are In Christ* (Gospel Coalition, 2019).
3. Charles Swindoll, *Growing Deep in the Christian Life: Essential Truths for Becoming Strong in the Faith* (Grand Rapids: Zondervan, 1995).

2. WHEN DID JESUS REALLY DIE ON THE CROSS?

1. Elyse Fitzpatrick, *Comforts from the Cross: Celebrating the Gospel One Day At A Time* (Wheaton: Crossway Books, 2009), 96-97.

3. HOW ARE YOU FILLING THAT GOD-SHAPED VOID?

1. C.S. Lewis, as quoted in *"C.S. Lewis: A Thought from a Quote in Mere Christianity."* In a May 23, 2006 blog by David Westerfield.
2. Augustine, *The Confessions of St. Augustine*. Various editions available.

3. C.S. Lewis, *Mere Christianity*. As quoted by Paul Tripp's email devotional, "Made for Another World," March 3, 2015.
4. Paul Tripp, *New Morning Mercies: A Daily Devotional* (Wheaton: Crossway Books, 2014), January 6 and 11 readings.

4. ARE YOU OVERLOADED AND STRESSED?

1. Paul Borthwick, as quoted by Aaron Schnoor in "Letting Your Soul Catch Up," in *The Intelligence of Everything*, October 2020.
2. Elisabeth Elliot Quotes on Facebook. Dec 11, 2016.
3. Ron Dunn, from a taped sermon I heard in the 1970s by this late pastor. Though this book is not the source of the quote, pastors will benefit from reading the biography written by Ron Owens: *Ron Dunn: His Life and Mission* (Innovo Publishing, 2020).
4. Mark Buchanan, *The Rest of God: Restoring Your Soul by Restoring Sabbath* (Thomas Nelson, 2007).
5. John Ortberg, *Soul Keeping: Caring for the Most Important Part of You* (Zondervan, 2014).
6. Richard Swenson, *Margin: Restoring Emotional, Physical, Financial and Time Reserves to Our Overloaded Lives* (NavPress, 2004).
7. Charles Hummel, *Tyranny of the Urgent: Revised and Expanded* (IVP, 1994).
8. Gordon MacDonald, *Ordering Your Private World: Revised and Updated Edition* (Thomas Nelson, 2017).
9. Richard Swenson, *Margin*, as quoted in Scotty Smith and Russ Masterson, *Searching for Grace* (Carol Stream: Tyndale House, 2021), 183.

5. DO YOU WANT TO STAY THE SAME?

1. From a chapel message by Bill Jones at Columbia International University.
2. Mark Buchanan, *Spiritual Rhythm: Being with Jesus Every Season of Your Soul* (Grand Rapids: Zondervan, 2010), 97-98.
3. Elyse Fitzpatrick, *Comforts from the Cross*, 59-60.

6. CAN YOU THANK GOD FOR PAIN?

1. Joni Eareckson Tada, *Beside Bethesda: 31 Days Toward Deeper Healing* (Colorado Springs: NavPress, 2014), 81.
2. Ibid, 168.

7. HOW IS SUFFERING A DIVINE GRACE?

1. Charles Spurgeon, as quoted in Zack Eswine's *Spurgeon's Sorrows* (Christian Focus Publications, 2014), 84, 86.

8. DO YOU NOTICE GOD'S MASTERPIECES?

1. Charles Spurgeon, "God Rejoicing in the New Creation" (Sermon #2211), as quoted in Randy Alcorn, *Happiness* (Carol Stream: Tyndale House, 2015), 282.

9. IS THAT A THERMOMETER IN YOUR MOUTH?

1. William Norris, as quoted in Charles Swindoll, *Growing Strong in Seasons of Life* (Grand Rapids: Zondervan, Reissue Edition, 1994).

10. DO YOU LISTEN WITH YOUR HEART?

1. As reported by Richard Peace and Thom Corrigan, *Learning to Care: Developing Community in Small Groups* (Littleton: Pilgrimage Training Group and NavPress,1995), 29.
2. Barbara Varenhorst, *Real Friends: Becoming the Friend You'd Like to Have* (Harper Collins, 1983).

11. ARE YOU WAVING A WHITE FLAG?

1. "First, Your Sword" devotional from RFTH Ministries (RightFromThe-Heart.org), August 28, 2010.
2. Scotty Smith and Russ Masterson, *Searching for Grace* (Carol Stream: Tyndale House, 2021), 102.

12. WILL YOU ASK GOD TO SEARCH YOUR HEART?

1. Paul Tripp, *New Morning Mercies*, February 14.

13. WILL YOU PRAY, "LORD, SEND A REVIVAL"?

1. "Revival Stories: The 1915 Gaza Land Revival," by Walton Yeun. May, 2021. Thinnkrevival.com Charlotte, N.C.
2. David Mains, from a message titled, "Enduring Characteristics of Revival," presented at a Ben Lippen conference held in Asheville, North Carolina in the mid-1980s.
3. An African American spiritual (Public Domain). The text appeared in James Weldon Johnson and J. Rosamond Johnson's *The Book of American Negro Spirituals*.
4. Nancy Demoss Wolgemuth, *Brokenness, Surrender, Holiness* (Chicago: Moody Press, 2008), 42.

14. IS "CONVICTING GRACE" AN OXYMORON?

1. I gleaned the quote from a novel by George MacDonald, Scottish author (1824-1905).
2. Charles Spurgeon, A-Z Quotes.
3. Joe Bayly, "Why Don't Sinners Cry Anymore?" *Eternity* (October, 1974), 71-72.
4. Elyse Fitzpatrick, *Comforts from the Cross*, 36.

15. HOW CAN YOU BEST GLORIFY GOD?

1. Charles Spurgeon, as quoted in John Piper, *Future Grace* (Sisters: Multnomah Books, 1995), 9.
2. John Piper, *Desiring God: Meditations of a Christian Hedonist* (Sisters: Multnomah Books, 2011), 144, 140.
3. Charles Spurgeon, as quoted in Piper, *Desiring God*, 140.

16. DOES GOD HIDE A SMILE BEHIND HIS DARK PROVIDENCE?

1. Elisabeth Elliot, *Suffering Is Never for Nothing* (Nashville: B&H Publishing, 2019), 23.

17. DO YOU WANT A MORE FRUITFUL MINISTRY?

1. Richard Foster, *Prayer: Finding the Heart's True Home* (San Francisco: Harper, 1992). From a chapter on intercessory prayer.

18. WHAT THREATENS THE SURVIVAL OF YOUR MARRIAGE?

1. Gary Thomas, *Sacred Marriage: What If God Designed Marriages to Make Us Holy More Than Happy?* (Grand Rapids: Zondervan, Reprint Edition, 2015).

19. HOW LONG SHOULD LOVE LAST?

1. From divorce.com. "*48 Divorce Statistics in the U.S. Including Divorce Rate, Race, and Marriage Length.*" January 3, 2023.
2. Ruth Graham, as quoted by Catherine Klasne in "*Divorce? No! Murder? Yes!*" blog on the website of Mediation Group (Upchurch Watson, White, & Max), 2023.

3. Tim Keller, *The Meaning of Marriage: Facing the Complexities of Commitment in the Wisdom of God* (Penguin Books, Reprint Edition, 2013).

20. DO YOU WANT GOD TO HEAL YOUR HEART?

1. Joni Eareckson Tada, *Beside Bethesda*.
2. Maurice Wagner, *The Sensation of Being Somebody: Building an Adequate Self-Concept* (Grand Rapids: Zondervan, 1975), 119.

21. HOW DOES GOD FLESH OUT HIS LOVE?

1. Ed Cunningham, as quoted by Just65.com, "Short Quotes for Your Best Friend."

22. WHY DO YOU NEED OTHER CHRISTIANS?

1. "Top 10 Facts That Make Redwood Trees Magnificent," in an online website for the Sempervirens Fund in Los Altos, California.
2. Watchman Nee, "Watchman Nee Quotes," Quotefancy.

23. WHAT IS THE MOST IMPORTANT SERMON YOU WILL EVER HEAR?

1. From a summary of Paul Tripp's viewpoint in a podcast titled, "Preach the Gospel to Yourself." A FaithPlay.com episode from "Theology Refresh: Podcast for Christian Leaders." April 5, 2014.

24. CAN YOU RELY ON HOW YOU FEEL?

1. Charles Spurgeon, *The Greatest Fight in the World* (Shawnee: Gideon House Books, 2016), 10.

25. DO YOU FEEL HOPELESS?

1. R.C. Sproul, DeeperChristianQuotes.com. "The Anchor of Hope," April 12, 2019.
2. Paul Tripp, *New Morning Mercies*, January 20.

26. WHO'S IN CONTROL WHEN LIFE HURTS?

1. Vaneetha Risner, *Dancing in the Rain* blog, "Is My Suffering Meaningless?" July 12, 2014.
2. Charles Spurgeon, in A-Z Quotes online.
3. Vaneetha Risner, *The Scars That Have Shaped Me: How God Meets Us in Suffering* (Desiring God, 2016).
4. Vaneetha Risner, *Walking Through Fire: A Memoir of Loss and Redemption* (Nashville: Thomas Nelson, 2021).
5. Joe Bayly, *The View from a Hearse: A Christian View of Death* (Warhorn Media 2014 edition). First released in 1969.
6. John Piper and Justin Taylor, Eds. *Suffering and the Sovereignty of God* (Crossway, 2006).
7. Paul Tripp, *New Morning Mercies,* January 2.

27. HOW DO YOU GO HIGHER WITH GOD?

1. Andrew Murray, from *Humility: The Journey Toward Holiness*, as quoted in Gary Rohrmayor's Your Journey Blog: "12 Priceless Quotes on Humility by Andrew Murray." August 12, 2014.

28. ARE YOU DISCOURAGED ABOUT YOUR WEAKNESSES?

1. Paul Tripp, *New Morning Mercies*, February 17.
2. James Packer, *Knowing God* (Downer's Grove: Intervarsity Press, 1973), 227.

29. DO YOU KNOW ANY HOMELESS PEOPLE?

3. John Mott, A-Z Quotes.
4. "What John Stott Said about the Social Justice Debate," a blog by Eric Geiger, October 11, 2018.

30. HOW WILL GOD USE YOU TO ENCOURAGE OTHERS?

5. David Olshine, *The Mystery of Silence: Making Sense of Life When God Seems Absent* (The Core Media Group, 2022).
6. John Maxwell, A-Z Quotes.

31. DO YOU WANT TO LIVE BEFORE YOU DIE?

7. *The Journals of Jim Elliot*, republished by Revell in 2002.
8. Peter Scazzero, *The Emotionally Healthy Church, Expanded Edition: A Strategy for Discipleship* (Grand Rapids, Zondervan, 2015).